Future Church
How Congregations Choose Their Character and Destiny

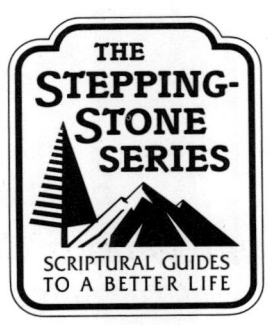

—to Life in the Spirit
   The Battle for Your Mind

—to Joy in the Home and Family
   Keeping Love in the Family

★—to Hope in the Church
   Future Church

Future Church

How Congregations Choose Their Character and Destiny

by
Leslie Parrott

Beacon Hill Press of Kansas City
Kansas City, Missouri

Copyright 1988
by Beacon Hill Press of Kansas City

ISBN: 083-411-2612

Printed in the United States of America

Cover: Royce Ratcliff

Permission to quote from the following copyrighted versions of the Scriptures is acknowledged with appreciation:

The New Testament in Modern English (Phillips), Revised Edition © J. B. Phillips, 1958, 1960, 1972. Used by permission of the Macmillan Publishing Co.

The *Revised Standard Version of the Bible* (RSV), copyrighted 1946, 1952, © 1971, 1973.

10 9 8 7 6 5 4 3 2 1

To

Andrew and Justin
adored grandsons
in the
fifth generation of
a church-loving family

Contents

Introduction   13

BOOK ONE:
CHOOSING OUR DIRECTION

1 / How Direction Decides Destiny   19

Scriptural Stepping-stones: Acts 11:22-26
"They sent forth Barnabas" • "With purpose of heart" • "Much people was added" • "The disciples were called Christians"

A Walk Through: What was the Church's original mission? • How can we know what our mission is today? • How can the local church find its direction in a secular, high-tech society?

2 / The Nature of God's Presence in the Church   37

Scriptural Stepping-stones: Eph. 2:19-22
"The household of God" • "Built upon the foundation" • "An holy temple" • "An habitation of God"

A Walk Through: What is the Church? • Who are the people of God? • What was the nature of God's presence in the Early Church? • Where and how does God manifest himself in the Church today?

Book Two:
Beyond Program and Planning

3 / Frustration and Fulfillment in the Church   55

Scriptural Stepping-stones: Matt. 16:13-20 "Whom say ye that I am?" • "Thou art the Christ" • "I will build my church" • "The keys of the kingdom"

A Walk Through: If the people in the church are really the people of God, why do they make me feel the way I feel? • If the Church is the Body of Christ, why are so many parts missing or damaged? • If we are really God's children, why do unchristian things happen in the church?

4 / Entering the Kingdom and Joining the Church   71

Scriptural Stepping-stones: Matt. 4:17—7:21 "The kingdom of heaven is at hand" • "The gospel of the kingdom" • "Enter into the kingdom" • "Thy kingdom come" • "Seek ye first the kingdom"

A Walk Through: What is the Kingdom? • Why did Jesus make the kingdom of God His main theme? • What is the difference between the Church and the kingdom of God?

Book Three:
Holiness Evangelism and Higher Education

5 / The Wesley Brothers and Holiness Evangelism   89

Scriptural Stepping-stones: Acts 2:1-6
"All with one accord" • "All . . . in one place" • "It filled all the house" • "They were all filled" • "Every man heard them speak"

A Walk Through: Who were the Wesley brothers and why are they so important to us? • What was the turning point in Wesley's evangelism from an impotent to a powerful ministry? • What is the ultimate goal in evangelism? • How important is evangelism to the future church?

6 / Holiness and the Educated Person   105

Scriptural Stepping-stones: Isa. 26:3; Luke 10:27; Heb. 8:10; Rom. 12:2; 8:6
"Whose mind is stayed on [the Lord]" • "Thou shalt love the Lord . . . with all thy mind" • "I will put my laws into their mind" • "Be ye transformed by the renewing of your mind" • "Carnally minded is death" • "Spiritually minded is life and peace"

A Walk Through: Religious characteristics of a holiness college • Wesley and reason • The skills of an educated mind • Tension between Christian theology and the secular attitude • The tendency to totally Christianize the curriculum • Authoritarian instruction • Church and denominational commitment

BOOK FOUR:
CONTINUING CONCERNS IN THE CHURCH

7 / Future Shock   **119**

Scriptural Stepping-stones: Acts 28:11-16
"We departed in a ship" • "We fetched a compass" • "We went toward Rome" • "[We] thanked God, and took courage" • "We came to Rome"

A Walk Through: The meaning of future shock • The impact of change • Change and physical sickness • The local church and its ability to cope with change • Family breakdown, AIDS, alcohol and drug abuse • God's therapy for change

8 / Science and Faith   **129**

Scriptural Stepping-stones: 1 Cor. 2:12-16
"Know the things that are freely given to us of God" • "Comparing spiritual things with spiritual" • "The natural man receiveth not the things of the Spirit" • "Who hath known the mind of the Lord?" • "But we have the mind of Christ"

A Walk Through: Science has changed our lives • Science in peace and war • What is science? • How do scientists work? • Science in Bible days • Christians afraid of science

9 / Television and Mass Media   137

Scriptural Stepping-stones: 2 Tim. 4:1-4
"Be instant in season, out of season" • "Teachers, having itching ears" • "Turn away their ears from the truth" • "Turned unto fables"

A Walk Through: Television cannot be ignored • Television is the great separator • TV walls that separate us from one another • No TV show substitutes for going to church

10 / Racism in the Church   145

Scriptural Stepping-stones: Luke 10:25-28; Col. 3:11
"A certain lawyer stood up" • "What is written in the law?" • "Thy neighbour as thyself" • "There is neither Greek nor Jew" • "But Christ is all, and in all"

A Walk Through: Even in the same race, the minority seem to suffer • What is racism? • The roots of racism • A worldwide problem • The Bible and racism

Book Five:
The Local Church in an International World

11 / Dealing with Unjust Laws   153

Scriptural Stepping-stones: Rom. 13:1-7
"Be subject unto the higher powers" • "Be afraid of the power" • "For he beareth not the sword in vain" • "Tribute to whom tribute is due" • "Honour to whom honour"

A Walk Through: What makes a law just or unjust? • Christian options to unjust laws • The meaning and power of nonviolent resistance • The attitude of Jesus toward unjust laws

12 / Nuclear Destruction and/or Peace in Our Time 167

Scriptural Stepping-stones: Ps. 33:12-17
"The nation whose God is the Lord" • "The Lord looketh from heaven" • "There is no king saved by the multitude" • "A mighty man is not delivered by much strength" • "An horse is a vain thing for safety"

A Walk Through: This is a dangerous world • Understanding the seriousness of world politics • But everything is not dark • Responsibility in world affairs • Faith and ethics in politics • Christians with human values • Homes with old-fashioned virtue • The transforming power of Christ

Introduction

The church today is in transition. Outwardly we see changes in the architecture of the buildings and the layout of the parking lots. Behind church doors we find differences in the music, the format of the worship services, and the style of preaching. The changes extend to staffing, the need for multiple services, and the expansion of programs to meet people's needs.

The times we live in are the reason for these changes in the church. Both secular and religious television programming have made their impact on the way people think. High-tech society has flooded us with instant information. This overkill has resulted in a cultural breakdown of moral standards that has not left the church unscathed. The heartbeat of the church is suffering from a persistent case of arrhythmia. The heartbeat is irregular. Children are more sophisticated and grow up more quickly than their parents did. They face moral issues such as abortion, drugs, alcoholism, prayer in schools, and arms reduction. Our national agenda includes such diverse matters as human rights, terrorism, and separation of church and state.

America is no longer a manufacturing-based society that depends on assembly lines and smokestacks. We have entered an information age that is being developed on the microchip and caters to three front-runners: the robot, the computer, and the word processor. People in the next generation will need to be better educated than their parents just to have a working relationship with the future.

There is no way we can conduct business as usual in the local church if we are to meet the needs of people in our towns and cities. Some churches are slowly closing their doors while committees regroup for a fight to survive. Other churches are thoughtlessly turning to any method or idea someone, somewhere, has found "successful."

What is the future direction for the local church? Where do we turn? Christian humanism and charismatic Pentecostalism are new forces for the church to reckon with. We can't ignore their influence in the local body, but most often we hear their message through the electronic church. Every week a great number of television preachers espouse some kind of questionable doctrine. Unfortunately, many of us don't know the difference. Scriptural discernment has given way to simplistic answers.

This book is designed for personal reading and group study in congregations. I have not offered definitive answers on program. I don't believe program is our problem; direction is. These pages are an honest effort to discuss and define direction in the future church, the one your children and mine will continue to build.

LESLIE PARROTT

Future Church
*How Congregations Choose Their
Character and Destiny*

Book One

CHOOSING OUR DIRECTION

*A Point of View
on Book One:*

The future church that is effective in serving its community will be more concerned with its direction than its statistics. The nature of God's presence in the church will be its highest priority.

Chapter 1

How Direction Decides Destiny

Scriptural Stepping-stones

Then tidings of these things . . .
> came unto the ears of the church which was in Jerusalem: and *they sent forth Barnabas,* that he should go as far as Antioch. Who, when he came, and had seen the grace of God, was glad, and exhorted them all, that *with purpose of heart* they would cleave unto the Lord. For he was a good man, and full of the Holy Ghost and of faith: and *much people was added* unto the Lord.
>
> Acts 11:22-24, italics added throughout

* * *

Then departed Barnabas to Tarsus, . . .
> for to seek Saul: and when he had found him, he brought him unto Antioch. And it came to pass, that a whole year they assembled themselves with the church, and taught much people. And *the disciples were called Christians* first in Antioch.
>
> Acts 11:25-26

* * *

As we consider the condition of the church today and try to discern God's direction for its future, we should answer some basic questions. Why was the Church born? What was its original mission? In what ways was God's presence evidenced in the Early Church? Understanding God's purpose for the Church in its beginning is essential to avoid missing His plan for its future.

Peter Berger, a prominent contemporary sociologist, wrote *Rumor of Angels,* offering a starting place as we explore our questions: "The church's purpose is not its own. The church is in the world on the behalf of God, by whose grace it has been called into existence. Thus at the heart of the church's act of self-definition is a basic theological question: What is the nature of God's presence in the world?" (New York: Doubleday and Co., 1976).

We can only know the nature of God's presence in the world if we examine the nature of His presence within the Church when it was young. How can we be sure the church is headed in the right direction? There is only one reliable standard. As Hans Kung, in his monumental study *The Church,* says: "One can only know what the church should be now if one also knows what the church was originally" (New York: Doubleday and Co., n.d.).

We do not need to wear sandals, drink water from clay pots, and hold services in private homes to be like the Early Church. As the culture changes, so do the mode and the methods of the church change—even its moods. Do we need to ask the Holy Spirit to manifest himself as the sound of a rushing mighty wind or as tongues like dancing fire on the heads of us believers? These were the accessories, not the substance when the Church was born. Even if we could pray down dramatic signs and wonders, we would not be re-creating the Early Church. What we need to know is the nature of God's presence in the world then so that we may live for that same Presence now.

* * *

I see little of the church's strength invested in understanding and maintaining a New Testament direction for the future. Instead, we are like congregations riding in open convertibles with no rearview mirrors. We are more interested in viewing the passing scene in organized religion than we are in seeing where we came from or where we may be headed. If someone's church moves past us in passenger count, we react immediately. We analyze the successful program in the other church and decide what makes their machinery run better than ours or generate more new members than ours. We then copy, borrow, and otherwise appropriate the most visible parts of the system from the other "successful" congregation and overlook the main thrust of their engine. We borrow the accessories but seldom examine the drive shaft. As a result, we look like their church and act like their people with the consequences blurred. In time, this eclectic borrowing leads to a blurred identity, since we are patterned after others who do not share our heritage or feel a commitment to our mission.

Our preoccupation with the religious scene around us results in many long conversations among laymen and ministers on what is working and not working in the church. We are preoccupied with the most visible signs. If we believe good music builds the church, then we major in good music. If stories of "true confession" perk the ears of listeners, then we fill the sermon slot with story time. If theology puts people to sleep, then we shield them from doctrinal teaching. Unfortunately, following religious trends makes for a people who lack a sound theology. The result tends toward church services that vacillate between gales of guilt and warm, fuzzy feelings.

If you can't see enough of the passing parade of evangelical methods from where you are, there are scores of seminars, short courses, conventions, and gatherings you can pay to attend where the latest models in current ideas are offered complete with notebooks and cassettes. You can't possibly fail to get back the cost of travel, hotel, meals, and registration fee in the usable ideas that will set your church in the right direction, even increase its momentum.

Or, will they?

I just finished reading a book by a denominational leader who was fed up with the failure of his church to stem the tide of dwindling membership. There was more negative eloquence on the first page of his book than I have read in a long time. The remorse and regret he expressed in sanctified irony triggered the fast-forward mechanism in my mind, and I scanned the pages in search of the solutions he would offer for a very obvious problem.

When I reached the chapters on what to do about denominational deterioration, I was disappointed. All he had to offer were some rehabilitated methods that had worked for him years ago. Church renewal, theological integrity, and spiritual Presence were lost in an attractive display of ideas for circumventing the antitheological mind-set he saw in secular society. He seemed pleased to have found ways to get people into the church before they fully realized their spiritual involvement. I was impressed with his analysis of his church's problem but disappointed in his solutions.

Only a few days after I finished reading the book, I was seated at lunch next to a man who had pastored the largest church in the same denomination. He had received more members than any other pastor in the history of their movement including the founder. When I asked him about the book, he said he also had written a book about the same denomination. His book had only been out 60 days, and 40,000 copies were already sold. Turning squarely to look me in the face, he said, "And I did not say one negative thing about my church."

In one case, a pastor's eloquence characterized a denomination's deterioration. In the other case, the man who had pastored its largest congregation and enjoyed a national pulpit wrote about the same church without saying anything negative. One man offered new methods as the solution to dwindling membership. The other man, known for his charisma in preaching, saw his pulpit as the tool for holding back deterioration and sustaining membership. Both responses reminded me of an old aphorism, "If your only tool is a hammer, you tend to see all your problems as nails."

* * *

If we think management, methods, material means, or public charisma are the raw materials for building the kingdom of God, we are in the wrong business. Those were the tools Lee Iacocca used to rebuild the Chrysler Corporation.

There is not a successful enterprise in America that doesn't have a strategy for the future. The Business Schools of Harvard, Stanford, and the University of Chicago have great segments of teaching/learning time dedicated to the understanding of strategic planning. However, transplanting corporate management strategies into the Church is not the way God intended us to find the future direction for His witness on earth. I wonder what God thinks about consultants, action plans, and market studies heralded in His name. He must wonder whatever happened to the pattern He gave to His best people, Paul, John, James, and Peter, and to the written design for the Church they passed on to us.

Those tools—strategic management, scientific methods, material means (money), and public charisma—are the accessories in church work but not its spiritual drive shaft. The engine that generates the power to run the system is peculiarly oblivious to Iacocca's ways for renewal. If seminars on church growth, long-range planning, and church management were to be God's means for ushering in the millennium of the Kingdom, it would be here.

But it isn't!

God knows we've tried. But somehow, things aren't working out. Morale, in many places, is low. Anxiety over pastoral assignments is higher than it needs to be. Great numbers of churches aren't adding even one new member a year on profession of faith. We can change the methods again officially or unofficially, and modify the means, but in many places it will be like moving the chairs around on the deck of the *Titanic*. What we need is a new sense of direction that keeps us away from the hidden icebergs waiting to rip our invisible undersides. What we need is direction into the main spiritual channel where God's blessings in the church flow freely and with vigor.

For several years I have started most of my days with toast and coffee at a local eatery that specializes in breakfast.

I've been interested, over the years, in watching the religious orientation of some of the groups who regularly show up for breakfast at about the same time each morning. For instance, there is a Catholic priest with some of his faithful people who arrive like clockwork for a hearty meal immediately after their early morning Mass. There is a table of Christian Businessmen and Youth for Christ types who shuffle lots of paper in the course of their discussions. Sometimes there is a table surrounded by the Methodist pastors in our area. And then there's us.

The group with whom I eat breakfast varies according to who's in town and what their schedules demand. But it includes pastors of large congregations, denominational administrators, Christian college people, and some very keen laymen.

If conversations among the other religious groups are like ours, there is lots of sharing of local, regional, and denominational church news. The news update is usually followed by a free-flowing discussion on what's good or bad, wise or unwise, right or wrong about all this. Then we predict what is likely to happen next as a fallout from what is happening now in these church decisions, ecclesiastical events, personnel changes, and so on ad infinitum until it is time to break up the group and go to work.

Don't knock this coffee cup gathering. These conversations are often very stimulating. Any freshman psychology student knows people talk about what concerns them most. We love our church, and so we talk about it.

However, I've made several observations about these breakfast table conversations. *First,* it is easier to pass judgment on someone's situation when we are not personally involved in the responsibility or the consequences. *Second,* we usually express our opinions on partial information. One more fact often changes the entire picture and ameliorates feelings. *Third,* you don't have to believe a rumor to repeat it. And *fourth,* most of the solutions we have for the problems of the church can be divided into two classes:

There is always pressure from within and without to adapt to the changing times. I am amazed at the number of things that were considered wrong in the church where I grew up and are now widely accepted and practiced. I also observe that one inch of ground gained in adjusting to the values of the world always calls for another inch, and another, and another.

Second, there are solutions that call for tenaciously holding on to the past. There is something discomforting about seeing old ways pass away and new values and new ideas take their places. The full two-week, three-Sunday revival and the Sunday night hymn-sing after church are, in many places, quaint memories of a generation gone by. Pastors who still accept calls to churches through prayer rather than by on-site inspection with their wives are in a distinct minority. I can remember when choir robes were in controversy as well as television, Sunday newspapers, and the circus. I can also remember when the big theological issue among evangelicals was eternal security. Now I seldom hear it mentioned, as we fill our conversations with long discussions on tongues, humanism, the electric church, and the problems of evangelism.

Have we lost or gained in giving up the ways of our fathers and grandfathers? When power steering, automatic shift, and tinted glass were introduced by the auto industry, there were people who turned them down on the basis of safety. But retaining old-fashioned steering, standard gearshifts, and untinted windshields would not have kept us from killing and maiming more people on our highways last year than were ever slain in Vietnam. Blind commitment to the past is not the answer for the direction of the future church any more than is careless adjustment to the values of the changing culture.

Cultural adjustment has been a hallmark of liberal Protestantism for many years. From 1860 to 1900, when the Church faced the onslaught of ideas from Charles Darwin and Sigmund Freud, liberals simply adjusted and accepted. Today, liberal pastors and congregations have shifted their emphasis away from the gods of physical and social science to exert their energies in the arena of social action. They often campaign on the liberal side of issues such as abortion and school prayer. They certainly focus on legitimate issues such as hunger and human rights but may do so at the expense of preaching personal salvation through saving faith.

In the meantime, conservative Protestantism has been fighting like fury to hold on to the past. Our own denomination is a good example. In the shift from first- to second-generation leadership in the Church of the Nazarene, there was great concern over maintaining "the glory" often talked about and expressed by Dr. P. F. Bresee. Dr. Timothy Smith mentions this anxiety in his history of the first 25 years of the church, *Called unto Holiness, Volume 1*. In an effort to hold on to the past, they decided to "keep the glory down" and defined it. In the 1920s, a consensus developed for identifying "the glory" as consisting of three factors: (1) *Open demonstra-*

tion, or shouting. Preachers and laymen were encouraged to give full vent to their spiritual emotions even if services were interrupted. (2) *Legalism.* For instance, "Abstain from all appearance of evil" (1 Thess. 5:22) could be stretched over as many things as desired. If I were concerned over the evil connotation of pop in a bottle and you were not, then I was more spiritual than you, or at least I had the greater amount of "the glory." (3) *Inordinate denominational loyalty.* No memberships in Rotary or other service organizations were allowed to compete with church loyalty. Therefore, the Nazarenes of this era stayed away from service clubs. Membership in the local council of churches could be construed as a compromise or even agreement with the theological stance of liberal members. So interdenominational ministerial fellowship was avoided.

We need to be fundamental in our doctrine, and we certainly need "the glory" manifest in our lives and our churches. But efforts to stop the clock or turn back the calendar almost always fail in setting direction for the future church. Blind commitment to the past, or even the status quo, can be as misdirected and thoughtless as adaption to the secular present. An insatiable hunger for returning to the good old days when things were like God wanted them to be results in church agendas that are focused on men's priorities and not God's.

The Bible is clear that tradition can never take precedence over God's Word: "He answered and said unto them, Well hath Esaias prophesied of you hypocrites, as it is written, This people honoureth me with their lips, but their heart is far from me" (Mark 7:6). The passage continues, "And he said unto them, Full well ye reject the commandment of God, that ye may keep your own tradition. . . . making the word of God of none effect through your tradition, which ye have delivered: and many such like things do ye" (vv. 9, 13).

* * *

I am not sure that a simplistic division of Protestantism into liberal and conservative camps is an adequate picture of what is going on today in the church. Among conservative evangelicals there are at least three kinds of churches that focus on wrong targets. They think of themselves as evangelical or conservative, and in some ways they are. The Christian humanists and the charismatics seem to have purposes that compete with the secular world, while the ultraconservative church is sidetracked like an outdated steam engine that huffs and puffs but doesn't generate any movement.

First, there is the issue of Christian humanism, as represented in the self-esteem ministry of Dr. Robert Schuller and thousands of other lesser-known pastors. The essence of this ministry was set down in Dr. Schuller's book *Self-esteem: The New Reformation.* Its main thesis is: You can do anything with your life that you can visualize, and God will help you do it. That is a very attractive idea, which was first popularized by Ralph Waldo Emerson, followed by Henry Ward Beecher, Norman Vincent Peale, and brought to its current state of popularity by the ministry of Anaheim's Crystal Cathedral.

In interviews and from time to time in his preaching, Dr. Schuller talks about repentance, forgiveness, grace, and the Lordship of Jesus Christ. In my personal visits with him, I know he is a man who believes in the power of the Resurrection and is a pastor who works comfortably within the parameters of Reformed theology. He sees himself as a proclaimer of the New Testament gospel to the millions of nonchurched people who are turned off by traditional churches. I further believe he is a man of integrity.

However, for many millions, he is a proclaimer of "Glory to man in the highest, and on earth, peace of mind." Many people get the idea that God is available to help us do our thing. They hear the blessings of self-esteem but miss the message of sacrificial obedience in self-denial. They hear the story of people "who through faith subdued kingdoms, . . . stopped the mouths of lions, quenched the violence of fire." But they miss the golden hinge in the 11th chapter of Hebrews, which consists of two words, "And others." Others, who had just as much faith as the high achievers, "had trial of cruel mockings and scourgings, yea, moreover of bonds and imprisonment . . ." (vv. 32-40). The attraction for many who embrace Christian humanism is not the nearness of the kingdom of God but the belief that "I can do anything."

The second happening among conservatives is the rise of charismatic superchurches and television ministries. These movements have gained wide acceptance for speaking in tongues. They have taken the minimal references of Paul to "unknown" tongues and elevated the practice into a hallmark for the presence of the Holy Spirit. For many charismatics, speaking in tongues is a sign of spiritual superiority if not a prerequisite evidence for the work of the Holy Spirit in a believer.

The model for these charismatic preachers is Pastor Cho, a Korean in Seoul who leads the largest Protestant congregation in the world. He has taken his ministry into Japan and has more converts already than all the evangelical missionaries were able to win since that island was opened to the outside world. Pastor Cho's focus is almost entirely spiritual, and his method is the organizational genius of a vast grid of small groups who are led and supervised by church representatives. The church emphasizes evangelism, nights of prayer, and charismatic services.

It is easy to react to these charismatic churches by attacking them for sensationalism, emotionalism, materialism, and biblical myopia. It seems that division and confusion are the systematic results in any congregation where the tongues issue rises. Sometimes it is easier to *react* toward charismatics in anger than to *respond* to them with understanding and love. But whether the rest of Protestantism likes it or not, charismatic churches have demonstrated impressive church growth patterns in many countries of the world. At last count, the largest church in 37 of the 50 states in the United States was charismatic. They are here, and quite likely to stay.

Remember my reference to riding in the convertible with the top down watching the church scene go by? I suggested we get anxious and sometimes upset at any gospel vehicle that passes us or tends to threaten our self-image. Any local congregation or international denomination that shows more success than we do becomes the object of our analysis. If it works for them, then it will work for us. If the Baptists succeed with buses, should we all buy buses? If the independents are growing with big buildings and heavy promotional programs, should we dream about larger sanctuaries that may be filled only when we contract with "Christian celebrities" to fill them? If the followers of Pastor Cho are building great churches with their charismatic ways, maybe we should look for ways to emulate him without the tongues.

I have a feeling the next wave in church method could be charismatic services without tongues. Will our song leaders and Sunday night choirs give way to small platform worship teams equipped with guitars, drums, and microphones? Will hymnbooks give way to worship choruses and "spiritual songs" projected on screens? Will clapping, waving, and looking heavenward with closed eyes replace focus on the pulpit? Will the old-fashioned invitation be restyled into highly intense altar gatherings that favor concerted prayer for signs and wonders? This kind of charismatic service, particularly on Sunday nights, may not be coming our way, but I will not be surprised if it is. However, if we pattern ourselves after the charismatic service, we should be reminded that it is only an evidence of our ability to borrow. It is not a definitive answer to the direction for the future church.

Third, there are those complacent congregations and denominations in a no-growth mode who will be like outdated steam-engine churches. They will sit in the station huffing and puffing, trying to generate movement, straining every pipe and valve to move. But old-fashioned locomotives, regardless of how well they are preserved, are mostly nostalgic reminders of a former era, not something people take seriously for their day-to-day transportation needs. These steam-engine churches are like the Penn Central Railroad, which went broke trying to run trains, forgetting they were in the transportation business. They are congregations with well-preserved facilities, harmless pastors in black suits, and dwindling memberships of second- and third-generation families who are committed to the church in its location, and a church program like the one in force when they were growing up. Their only mission is to keep the church alive in the way it has always been. They shine the pipes and blow the whistle on Homecoming Sunday and leave the place in peace the rest of the year. About the only significant thing they do as a congregation is meet the budget, or at least report that they tried.

Churches who think the answer to today's challenge is to be like their fathers and grandfathers usually succeed in being like their fathers and grandfathers, but not much more. They miss the opportunity to help save a hellward-bound community. They don't see the people torn by the carnage of sin; scrambling to keep their children from destroying themselves in alcohol, drugs, and sex; sunk in the mire of materialism; and fighting for the survival of their marriages. Help for the lost in many communities will more likely come via the charismatic TV ministry or the Baptist bus. If sinners are converted in the complacent congregation, they are likely, in time, to leave for a "more alive" church. The year-end tally on new members by profession of faith will be very small.

What a pity. These doctrinally sound churches are bogged down with negativism, self-righteousness, legalism, and spiritual blindness. The community around them is bogged down in drugs, divorce, alcoholism, and all the other results of sin and spiritual insensitivity. The church and the community need each other, but it is not likely they will ever meet.

People in the steam-locomotive church believe in salvation by grace but just barely. They like services that focus on guilt instead of joy. The Ten Commandments are more attractive than the Beatitudes. They like Good Friday and the Cross more than Easter morning and the Resurrection.

Negativism expresses itself in a continual flow of criticism about nearly everything and everybody. Congregations turn all their psychic energies inward on each other, and so nothing happens out there where sinful people have needs. If someone new comes to a complacent church, he is likely to be taken in on suspicion while the church insiders examine their lives to identify likely inconsistencies. Most new people don't stay long.

Besides being negative and legalistic, these steam-locomotive churches are almost always dominated by one strong family. If that family is negative or legalistic, there is not much the church can do besides huff and puff.

Family-owned businesses have a hard time attracting good talent because capable people do not like being dominated by one strong figure who will always favor sons and daughters when cross-purposes develop. Because the working world out there is filled with opportunities for talented people, they just move on. The same thing happens in the church that is dominated by one family intermarried with connections that would rival the ancient kings of Britain and Europe. Good people newly converted or just arrived in the community will not subject themselves to the inevitable abuses that come in a family-dominated, negatively oriented, small church. The world of Christian churches is just too full of other options.

The effective churches I know about have been able to put themselves beyond negativism, legalism, and the domination of one strong family. These churches are no longer bogged down in issues most Christians don't care about. People are fulfilled in a congregation of loving, caring brothers and sisters in the Lord who still hear the gospel as good news and see the Holy Spirit as a Person and not just a theological explanation. They experience the Holy Spirit as a Comforter and not an event. In the effective church, holiness is not a slogan in the literature but a positive, clean, Christian lifestyle. Sanctification is both an instantaneous experience and a lifelong process. And membership in the human race is not off-limits.

* * *

But all this discussion about what the church is like in the cities and hamlets of our world does not answer the question on the nature of God's presence in the world today. What is the right direction for the future church? The message of Christian humanism, the charismatic ways of worship, or the church with the locomotive complex are not the answers.

We will find direction in our own understanding of the church in the New Testament. The Church did not come into being on its own. God called the Church out of the world as a gathering of the Body of believers. The history of the Church is the story of its pilgrimage through 20 centuries of cultural changes and circumstances that refuse to stand still. To keep our direction straight for today and tomorrow, God has given us a guide, just as He did the Israelites in the wilderness—a pillar of cloud by day and a pillar of fire by night. *Our guide is the Word of Christ as reported in the New Testament.* With the presence of Christ above and beneath it, behind and before it, the Church is headed in the right direction.

In Christ's Church, numbers are not as important as direction. Jesus talked about what happens when two or three are gathered together. He also ministered to throngs like the 5,000 men and their hungry families. Jesus invested most of

His ministry in 12 men, and at the end there were only 120 gathered in an upper room to talk about what to do next.

We do not need an evangelism explosion as much as we need a direction for evangelism. Church growth should come in support of the church's direction, not running ahead of it. The church is in the world on behalf of God. The church is the dwelling place of the Holy Spirit. He is providing its energy and direction.

The only way the church can know how to go forward is to return to the original pattern. The New Testament Church is not something to emulate in custom. The world moves on. These are not New Testament times. The New Testament does not open with a doctrine of the Church. But it gives us direction and tells us the nature of God's presence in the world.

The purpose of this chapter:
To examine the options for choosing direction in the future church.

QUESTIONS FOR THOUGHT AND DISCUSSION

1. What are some characteristics of a liberal church?
2. What is Christian humanism?
3. Is it possible to be charismatic or Pentecostal and not speak in tongues?
4. What are the characteristics of the complacent, no-growth church?
5. What is the nature of God's presence in the world today?
6. What seems to be the direction of our church?

Chapter 2

The Nature of God's Presence in the Church

Scriptural Stepping-stones

Now therefore ye are . . .

> no more strangers and foreigners, but fellowcitizens with the saints, and of *the household of God;* and are *built upon the foundation* of the apostles and prophets, Jesus Christ himself being the chief corner stone; in whom all the building fitly framed together groweth unto *an holy temple* in the Lord: in whom ye also are builded together for *an habitation of God* through the Spirit.
>
> Eph. 2:19-22

* * *

The word *church* means different things to different people. For some people, *church is a building:* "I'll meet you at the church," where we go for religious activities. The oldest existing church building in the world is in Syria, built in the fourth century, after the Emperor Constantine made Christianity the official religion of the Roman Empire. From then until now, Christians have been constructing church buildings, designing them to fit their style of worship and the historical setting of the times. But a church is much more than a building.

For some people, *church is a place for activity with other Christians:* "Our church softball team is a winner." Some churches have erected signs calling themselves Christian Centers, as if to distance themselves from the negative concept of a church they think is in the minds of many people. The church does need accessibility, visibility, and identity, but the church is more than a Christian activity center.

For other people, *church is a congregation made up of homogeneous units:* "All our friends go to our church." This is a group or groups of like-minded people who enjoy each other, usually because they are the same color, come from the same socioeconomic strata, and have similar interests. And it is only a small step from this concept to a clublike atmosphere that is hard for newcomers to access. Homogeneous units develop naturally by attracting people of like-mindedness and eliminating people with a difference. But the church is more than a group of like-minded people.

Some people even see *church as a business* with assets, liabilities, income, expenditures, a board of directors, all designed to serve the membership, who constitute the stockholders and the customers: "How much equity does your church have in its plant?" In this concept, the programs of the church are wholly owned subsidiaries of the board, which is the holding company. Some churches are developing a new place on the staff for a layman called "president." The church does have many responsibilities that need to be expedited in a businesslike manner. But the church is more than a business.

Particularly in this day of television ministries, some people see *church as a great gathering of people:* "Half of our church are people from other churches," who may meet in the civic auditorium or an athletic arena. Churches do have audiences, and sometimes there are large congregations, but there is more to a church than the gathering of people.

The English word *church* in the original language means *"that which belongs to the Lord."* This New Testament word *church* was used by Jesus, who said, "Upon this rock I will build my church" (Matt. 16:18). There is a closely related word, *ecclēsia,* from which we get the word *ecclesiastical. Ecclēsia* refers to "the people who belong to the Lord." Although *ecclēsia* is used 115 times in the New Testament, the concept is repeated many more times. Usually *ecclēsia,* in the ancient world, referred to people who had been called out by a herald to meet in a public place for some special purpose. *The Church, then, are those who have been called out of the world to be the people of God.*

This idea of the Church as the people of God was in the mind of Paul when he addressed his first Corinthian letter to "the church of God which is at Corinth, to them that are sanctified . . ." (1:2). When Paul gave his farewell message to the Ephesian elders who had come down to meet him at the harbor in Miletus, he urged these church leaders to be good "overseers, to feed the church of God, which he hath purchased with his own blood" (Acts 20:28). The church is not a congregation of joiners. It is the people of God who have been called out from the world. They are in the world, surrounded by the world, and faced by the world, but not of the same spirit as the world.

The Church is also the Temple of the Holy Spirit and the Body of Christ. As Christ was God's Temple, we, the Church, are His. In the Old Testament, the Tabernacle was the place where God chose to meet with His people. The Tabernacle was the place where God's glory shone, where priests made sacrifice for sin. The Tabernacle was the place where the people of God gathered to study His law and to learn His will.

But the Tabernacle as an institution became an impediment to the purposes of God. Jesus entered the Temple with great anger because the house of prayer had become "a den of thieves" (Matt. 21:13). It had been destroyed centuries earlier, was later rebuilt, and then was destroyed again.

The Old Testament Temple was replaced by the body of Christ. Jesus prophesied, saying there would "not be left here one stone upon another, that shall not be thrown down" (Matt. 24:2). Hearing this, the Jews accused Jesus of saying He could literally destroy the Temple. Jesus made things even worse for himself when He said, "Destroy this temple, and in three days I will raise it up" (John 2:19). These statements were absurd to the Jews who misunderstood them and believed Jesus was talking about destroying and rebuilding the physical Temple in Jerusalem.

But Jesus was saying that the Temple was no longer the structure of stone that stood before them. It was His own body, which they were preparing to destroy. But this body of Christ would be raised up into new life on the third day as the Temple of God.

In Jesus, every relationship between a holy God and sinful man was to be established and maintained. When Jesus died, the curtain in the Temple that shrouded the holy of holies in sanctified mystery was ripped from top to bottom. This tearing of the veil made the way into God's presence direct, no longer through the holiest place in the Temple but through the crucified and risen body of Jesus Christ. The true Temple of God is the risen Lord.

In the New Testament, the Church is repeatedly called the Temple of God or God's house. When Paul wrote the church at Corinth, he said, "Know ye not that ye are the temple of God, and that the Spirit of God dwelleth in you? If any man defile the temple of God, him shall God destroy; for the temple of God is holy, which temple ye are" (1 Cor. 3:16-17).

This New Testament idea of the Church as the Temple of God is even clearer in Paul's letter to the church in Ephesus: "In whom all the building fitly framed together groweth unto an holy temple in the Lord: in whom ye also are builded together for an habitation of God through the Spirit" (2:21-22).

The unknown writer of Hebrews also saw the Church as the Temple of God: "Having therefore, brethren, boldness to enter into the holiest by the blood of Jesus, by a new and living way, which he hath consecrated for us, through the veil, that is to say, his flesh; and having an high priest over the house of God; let us draw near with a true heart in full assurance of faith, having our hearts sprinkled from an evil conscience, and our bodies washed with pure water" (10:19-22).

Even in the Revelation of John, the idea of the Church as the Temple of the Holy Spirit continues strong: "Him that overcometh will I make a pillar in the temple of my God ... He that hath an ear, let him hear what the Spirit saith unto the churches" (3:12-13).

Closely related to the idea of the Church as the Temple of God is the concept of the Church as *"the Body of Christ."* This reference to the people of God is used many times in the writings of Paul.

Although the church at Rome was gathered from many nations in the Middle East and included both Jews and Gentiles, Paul writes them, "So we, being many, are one body in Christ, and every one members one of another" (12:5).

I wonder what the Christians in Corinth—the Hollywood of ancient Greece—thought the first time Paul's first letter was read to them: "That there should be no schism in the body; but that the members should have the same care one for another. And whether one member suffer, all the members suffer with it; or one member be honoured, all the members rejoice with it. Now ye are the body of Christ, and members in particular" (12:25-27).

Paul also exalts the Church as Christ's Body in his letter to the Ephesians, "And hath put all things under his feet, and gave him to be the head over all things to the church, which is his body, the fulness of him that filleth all in all" (1:22-23).

Again, in the same letter Paul says, "For we are members of his body, of his flesh, and of his bones" (5:30).

The Colossian Christians lived far inland from the port city of Ephesus. But Paul's message on the Church as the habitation of Christ was still the same: "For by him were all things created, that are in heaven, and that are in earth, visible and invisible, whether they be thrones, or dominions, or principalities, or powers: all things were created by him, and for him: and he is before all things, and by him all things consist. And he is the head of the body, the church: who is the beginning, the firstborn from the dead; that in all things he might have the preeminence" (1:16-18).

Jesus sent His Holy Spirit to live in believers. The church, then, is the fellowship of those who believe and receive His Spirit, even if there are only two or three gathered in His name (Matt. 18:20). Regardless of size, location, color, or name on the door, the church is a gathering of those in whom God's Spirit dwells.

God's presence was poured out on five gatherings in Acts, beginning with Pentecost and concluding with the church at Ephesus, but always on groups or congregations of people. We believe in the personal experience of God's sanctifying grace through the Holy Spirit, but we also believe, on the basis of Acts, that the Spirit dwells in the Church as the Temple of the Holy Spirit (Acts 2; 4; 8; 10; 19).

If the Church is the dwelling place of God's Spirit, then certainly the Early Church should be a good working model for us. The Holy Spirit was alive in the first churches; His presence is the same today.

* * *

What conclusions can we draw from the New Testament *ecclēsia? The church is not a disconnected, egocentric, isolated, independent, self-sufficient religious organization.* The church is the fellowship of believers who meet regularly in a given place for the purpose of exalting Christ the risen Lord. In this fellowship, Christians express their gratitude to God and to each other as members of the Body of Christ on earth. In this fellowship, Christians receive support for their faith, strength for their daily lives, and motivation for Christian service.

The church is fully the church in every hallowed place where believers systematically gather. The local church is not a section of the whole church, which is bigger and more important than the local congregation. The church is both local and worldwide. It exists wherever the smallest congregation of no more than two or three are gathered regularly in His name for worship, study, and service. The church does not exist in the denominational headquarters; on the campuses of its colleges, universities, and seminaries; or in the publishing house where its literature is created. The denominational structure, the learning institutions, and the publishing house are connected to the church and sustained for the purpose of serving the local congregation. And something is grossly wrong when regional and general offices, educational institutions, and publishing houses have a life of their own separate from dedicated service to the local churches. The church is the place where the gospel is preached, the Lord's Supper is served, new converts are baptized, and the gifts and ministries of the people are used.

The local churches are connected by a divine calling. They gain their strength from a doctrinal heritage, unique features in worship, Christian life-style, and other spiritual and cultural cords, including vast networks of families and friends. But all of the local churches together, worldwide, are no more the church than each congregation that meets regularly, whether the gathering be under a thatched roof in some equatorial third world country, in an expansive auditorium of a very large metropolitan congregation, or in some quaint church house in a small hamlet. The church does not exist as the sum total of all the people in the local congregations, nor can the church be broken down into the number of existing congregations. The church exists fully in each place where believers have chosen to gather. There is not a Corinthian church, or the First Church of Corinth, but "the church of God which is at Corinth" (1 Cor. 1:2; 2 Cor. 1:1). Each congregation regardless of size or importance is a full and perfect manifestation of the *ecclēsia,* the people who are called out from the world. Each church is a prototype of "the general assembly and church of the firstborn" (Heb. 12:23).

The Church is more than the sum of its members. The Church does not exist in the free association of the people who have joined the fellowship. The Church exists in response to the call of God. In spite of its institutionalism and human failure, the Church is the foundation and creation of God. God provided the Tabernacle in the wilderness and the Temple in Jerusalem for His people. When men became so wayward that the functions of Temple worship failed to reconcile them to God, He allowed the Temple to be destroyed.

God provided His own Son to live among men. God allowed Him to die on a cross as though He were personally responsible for our sins. Then God raised Jesus from the grave as the ultimate Victor over both sin and death. Seven weeks and one day after the resurrection of Jesus, God poured out the fullness of the Holy Spirit on 120 believers who were gathered in Christ's name. The Church was born. God moved at every critical point in its preparation, birth, and life. It is His Church. Someday, when the time is right, the Church will be called again, this time for the triumphal entry into His eternal presence and the consummation of this age.

If the Church is God's own, what is the nature of His presence there?

God's presence is alive today in the authority of the Scriptures. There was no New Testament in existence when the Church was born. For most of their lives, the first generation of the Church had only the Old Testament translated into Greek, which was the international language of business in that day as English is today. However, as the apostles began to age, and time was running out for those who had known Jesus in the flesh, the Church began to collect the writings that eventually became the New Testament canon. The first collections began with the letters of Paul. Then came the Synoptic Gospels (Matthew, Mark, and Luke), the Acts of the Apostles, other letters, and finally the writings of John's Gospel and the Revelation.

The writings contained in our New Testament were chosen by the Church in the first centuries (under the direction of the Holy Spirit) because these documents had the ring of God's authority. As Christ was the Living Word (John 1:1), the New Testament wedded to the Old Testament became the norm and guideline for the Church.

The New Testament writings did not fall from heaven. They were not the work of religious ecstatics filled with spiritual madness. The writers were not divine secretaries who simply sat passively transcribing the dictation of God. The New Testament is the result of very human writers who were fully inspired by the Holy Spirit to write with authority and infallibility. This is why their writings are filled with both hope and judgment, and are sharper than any two-edged sword, given for both comfort and reproof. God's presence is manifest in the authority of the Scriptures.

This leaves one big question: *How can the local church give the authority of God's Word more meaning among the congregation?* The Bible needs to be read aloud by the pastor and people. Any service without the public reading of the Bible is omitting one of the most important ways God uses to manifest His presence.

The Bible must be studied beginning in childhood. As the first six grades in public school (ages 6-12) are given to the mastery of the skills of reading, writing, and arithmetic, so the same six years can be dedicated in Sunday School and church to the mastery of the narrative content of the Bible. The junior high and high school years at church are the time for exposure to basic Christian theology, Christian ethics, and churchmanship, along with the practical matters of Christian relationships. With this foundation, a lifelong study of the Word is under way with increments of help each week in public worship, personal devotions, and group discussions.

One important distinction needs to be made between a church that centers on personal religious experience and a church that focuses on the authority of the Bible. Churches that focus on personal experience are given to frequent pulpit calls for "a new touch" or an updating of Christian experience. These churches tend to keep guilt feelings alive in good people by preaching standards of devotion and Christian service that are unrealistic except for the short run. This kind of church can drift toward fanaticism on the one side or liberalism on the other as changing leadership adjusts to the idea of coping with local expectations. Christian stability suffers when the focus is on personal experience because emotions rise and fall. It takes a steady hand to carry a full cup.

The church that focuses on the authority of the Word will tend to be less concerned about the content in personal experience and more concerned about willful acceptance of New Testament promises and theology. The Billy Graham organization, Campus Crusade, Youth for Christ, and many churches related to their work find more ground for salvation in the authority of God's Word than in the immediacy of Christian experience. Spiritual counseling is done with a Bible in a prayer room, while experience-centered conversions are more often at a public altar in an atmosphere of spiritual encouragement generated by emotion-filled prayers and spiritual songs.

Actually, there need not be a focus on one of these above the other, but a balance between them. The nature of God's presence is manifest in His Word. God is present in His promise to forgive sins. God is present in the theology for spiritual cleansing of the sinful nature. And He is manifest in the faith that provides us the power to live by. Confidence in His Word constitutes the ground for the fullness of a personal relationship with our Lord.

The nature of God's presence is manifest in the power of Christ's resurrection.

One of the most important scriptures in the theology of the Church is 1 Corinthians 15. The entire chapter can be summarized in a few words: *Without the Resurrection, there can be no Church.* "If there be no resurrection of the dead, then is Christ not risen: and if Christ be not risen, then is our preaching vain, and your faith is also vain" (vv. 13-14).

Jesus announced no public intention to organize and establish a church. He talked privately with Peter and the other disciples about the rock on which He would build His kingdom. He never based His preaching on a remnant of believers who would begin an organization. When He talked about the kingdom of God, He set forth no requirements beyond receiving salvation and submitting one's will to God.

For all the New Testament writers, the church is conditioned on the death and resurrection of Christ. The first Christians did not speak or write about a church until after God raised Jesus from the dead. The church is a post-Easter happening. It came into existence when men and women began gathering on Sunday mornings in selected homes to celebrate the Resurrection.

Millions of people in the world today still believe in the Resurrection for very understandable reasons:

There is a disarming honesty in the reports on the Resurrection in the Gospels. The reporters who wrote about the Resurrection made no effort to harmonize their accounts. That really does not matter, for these were not police reports. They based their writings on what they had experienced and what was told them by other on-the-spot witnesses. If they had completely harmonized their stories, collusion would have been obvious. But on one fact they all agree: "He is risen!"

The evidence of the Resurrection was enough to convince a city of doubters. The entire religious and civil establishment in Jerusalem did all they could to hush and otherwise refute the Resurrection story. The Resurrection was first an incredible whisper among amazed groups, but 50 days after it took place, there were 3,000 people in one day who believed Peter when he said, "This Jesus hath God raised up, whereof we all are witnesses" (Acts 2:32). There were people in Jerusalem who wanted nothing more than to discredit the story of Christ's resurrection. They paid soldiers to lie about what happened to the stone and the body. If Peter's message could have been refuted, there were men in high places who would have done it, but they could not. The Resurrection is a fact of our faith.

Resurrection faith changed the lives of the disciples. Nothing but the Resurrection could explain such a sudden and radical change in these men. Peter, who followed afar off in fear, became bold when the Spirit sent him into the streets of Jerusalem, talking openly of Christ and proclaiming His resurrection. The lives of these men were not transformed by the invention of a myth. Men do not endure martyrdom for a charade.

Faith in the Resurrection has given the Church its persistent vitality. When the Church swept out of Jerusalem in the conquest of the world, the Resurrection message was its central theme. If Christ were not risen, the Church would have died long ago. The Resurrection as a fact of our faith is still the centerpiece in the message of the Church.

There is power in the risen Lord to change men's lives today. Malcolm Muggeridge, a British writer and television personality, was converted doing a documentary on the life of Jesus. He was a staunch nonbeliever, a man without faith, until the end of the series when he walked with the crew from Jerusalem to Emmaus. A spark of faith blossomed during that journey. And like Cleopas and his companion, Malcolm Muggeridge also returned to Jerusalem saying, "The Lord is risen indeed . . . Did not our heart burn within us, while he talked with us by the way . . . ?" (Luke 24:34, 32). Since that day on the Emmaus road, Malcolm Muggeridge has become a strong force for Christ in Britain. Some have said his Christian influence has been greater than the archbishop of Canterbury. While I listened to him relate his experience with Christ, I thought, Here is a man whose faith and witness is based on the fact he actually believes, without question, in the resurrection of our Lord.

There are three observations to be made on the power of the Resurrection in our local churches: (1) It meets the needs of the most guilty person among us, such as Mary Magdalene. (2) It transforms the life of the person who has been disappointed in religious experience, such as the two on the Emmaus road. (3) It answers the questions of the most persistent doubter, such as Thomas.

The nature of God's presence is manifested wherever His love is practiced. I attended a seminar more than a decade ago where I learned a definition of the church that has stuck with me until now. The minister in charge was a hyperactive fellow with a sanctified ego as big as all outdoors, and dramatic enough to be on stage. But in spite of these human factors, he had spent a lot of time figuring out what makes a church grow, and he was surrounded by proof that what he believed in worked. He said that a church was "a caring, sharing, loving fellowship of people who meet together in the name of Christ." This was mostly a working definition, for he used each key word—caring, sharing, loving, fellowship—as keys for implementing the very forceful program he had developed for church growth.

In many ways this functional definition is excellent. Applying it will get results. But theologically the definition falls short because caring, sharing, and fellowship all flow from one source, which is love. Have you ever been in a church where there was no presence of love? A service club meeting can have fellowship. But when love becomes the dominant attitude and emotion in a fellowship, wonderful things begin to happen. New people come to church, and they want to stay. Workers are recruited easily. The feelings of people are less touchy. Forgiveness flows openly. Attitudes turn toward the positive. Personal finance and church finance move closer to one another.

With love, and not just orthodoxy, a new kind of fellowship develops that transforms every relationship, both human and divine. Among believers there are many differences but few distinctions. In Christ, the broken relationship between man and God is restored in love. Because of His love, we also become "members one of another" (Rom. 12:5). Christ's love can overcome the barriers men have erected between themselves and God, and between each other. "This is his commandment, That we should believe on the name of his Son Jesus Christ, and love one another" (1 John 3:23).

The purpose of this chapter:
To examine the nature of God's presence among the early Christians as a guide to the future church.

QUESTIONS FOR THOUGHT AND DISCUSSION

1. What does the word *church* mean to you?
2. What is a homogeneous unit in a church?
3. Who are the *ecclēsia?*
4. How is the nature of God present in His Word?
5. What does the "love of God" mean to you?
6. How does the power of the Resurrection matter to the church today?

Book Two

BEYOND PROGRAM AND PLANNING

*A Point of View
on Book Two:*

> The future church that is effective in serving its people will come to peace with itself as the source of the people's greatest joy while also serving as the source of their greatest frustrations. The church and the kingdom of God are not the same. Jesus preached the kingdom of God, but what we got was the church, highly organized and fully institutionalized.

Chapter 3

Frustration and Fulfillment in the Church

Scriptural Stepping-stones

When Jesus came . . .

> into the coasts of Caesarea Philippi, he asked his disciples, saying, *Whom do men say that I the Son of man am?* And they said, Some say that thou art John the Baptist: some, Elias; and others, Jeremias, or one of the prophets.
>
> Matt. 16:13-14

* * *

He saith unto them, . . .

> *But whom say ye that I am?* And Simon Peter answered and said, *Thou art the Christ, the Son of the living God.* And Jesus answered and said unto him, Blessed art thou, Simon Barjona: for *flesh and blood hath not revealed it* unto thee, but my Father which is in heaven. And I say also unto thee, That thou art Peter, and upon this rock *I will build my church;* and the gates of hell shall not prevail against it. And I will give unto thee *the keys of the kingdom* of heaven: and whatsoever thou shalt bind on earth shall be bound in heaven: and whatsoever thou shalt loose on earth shall be loosed in heaven.
>
> Matt. 16:15-19

Then charged he his disciples . . .
> that they should tell no man that he was Jesus the Christ.
>
> Matt. 16:20

* * *

Most of us are so deeply involved in the church that excommunication would be like physical dismemberment. Taking the church from our lives would be like cutting off an arm or leg. For many of us the church is so important to our sense of well-being we would need an emotional wheelchair without it.

There are reasons for this dependency. Many of us were born in Nazarene parsonages and learned to depend on the church for our physical needs even before we were aware of our spiritual and social needs. Others of us were born into the homes of wonderful Christian laymen who brought us to the altar of the church for dedication or baptism when we were infants. Still others of us came to the church when the experiences of life began to turn against us. And we found in the church a spiritual and social home for this world and the world to come. For many of us, the church is our extended family.

When the artist starts to weave a beautiful tapestry, the work begins with an ordinary piece of cloth spun from hemp or flax. Then, with the pattern and threads that have been chosen, the artist begins to weave. There is an analogy between the process of the tapestry and the process of our lives. Our lives begin with an ordinary piece of cloth. Then, with the beautiful threads and the pattern God has chosen, He begins to weave the tapestry of our lives. And for most of us, the threads of our lives are so interwoven in our church that the pattern would fall apart if those threads ever came unraveled.

To help make my point, I'll be autobiographical. I was born in a Nazarene parsonage next door to the church at 9:30 on Sunday morning, probably in time to be counted in Sunday School. My first recollection of the church is sitting on my mother's knee on the front row while my father was asking all of the adults to take small children on their laps so the people could be seated who were still standing. All of my early childhood memories are related to the church. I remember great revivals with people like Bud Robinson and R. T. Williams and camp meetings with the Vaughn Radio Quartet, C. B. Fugett, and the brothers John and Bona Fleming. The biggest event for me in the entire summer was the Sunday School picnic. Another close rival was the annual all-church fish fry on the banks of the Sangamon River. It was the only time in the entire year when I had all of the ice-cold soda pop and watermelon I could eat. We enjoyed the Sunday School attendance drives and looked forward to seeing whether the reds or the blues would win. We enjoyed Vacation Bible Schools and choir and orchestra practices. I first learned to transpose on sight by playing a horn in a church orchestra.

But that is not all. While I was standing in registration line as a freshman at Olivet, I saw a young woman about 5 feet 2 inches tall wearing a yellow sweater and a pink plaid skirt with bobby socks and saddle shoes. She really caught my eye! We played tennis that afternoon and then went to the Wagon Wheel for a milkshake. I learned she had the same heroes in the church I had, and the friends her family enjoyed were the same friends our family enjoyed. Some years later, after we left Olivet Nazarene College, we made a calculated decision to bury our lives in the Church of the Nazarene. We have lived in Nazarene houses, driven Nazarene automobiles, eaten Nazarene food, read Nazarene books, and written Nazarene books. We have thought like Nazarenes and dressed like Nazarenes. Our highest family goal was to raise our three boys to enjoy the same standards and priorities we had accepted in the church.

What I have said about myself and our family could be said about hundreds of thousands of Christians. We all love the church and are committed to it. But there is a paradox that exists in our relationship with the church and its members.

While the church is our greatest source of fulfillment, it is also our greatest source of frustration. Anytime you give yourself completely to any one person or organization, that person or organization can both bless you and hurt you. Peter Drucker said that the person who gives himself completely and absolutely to the organization is defenseless before its inevitable disappointments. And Abraham Maslow said, "No relationship is ever free from the twin factors of cooperation and competition." This idea surfaces in the family of God just as it does in the family at home.

Sometimes I get the feeling that I have been married so long that maybe I was just born married. This is true because I cannot think of my life separate from my wife. She is the other half of me. But just because my life is deeply and emotionally involved in hers, and hers in mine, she can do more for me than any other person in the world. Just a smile can make me feel better when I am down. Or a word fitly spoken can restore my sagging confidence, put a new spring in my heel, and a new look of optimism on my face. But at the same time, she can destroy my self-esteem more quickly than anyone else in the world. Let me remind you again that it is a risk to commit yourself fully to anyone. But the alternative is even worse. And that is true in the church just as it is in marriage.

For years I thought my frustrations came because the church failed to live up to its own standards. Then I learned something about the church that put me at peace and made me understand and love it all the more.

The passage of Scripture that helps me the most in this regard is Matt. 16:13-20, which has its source in Mark and is repeated again in Luke.

Jesus went with His disciples 25 miles north and east of the Sea of Galilee to a place called Caesarea Philippi. Here, at a spot about 1,700 feet up the side of the mountain, under the towering majesty of snowcapped Mount Hermon, Jesus made His first great proclamation about the Church. In light of the current international events, the place where He spoke is even more dramatic. Jesus stood inside a triangle that runs from Jerusalem to Damascus and from Damascus to Beirut and back to Jerusalem. And here in this internationally sensitive area, He talked with His disciples about building His Church. Here is a loose paraphrase of what happened.

Having arrived at the foot of the mountain, Jesus sat with His disciples, perhaps around a campfire to ward off the chilly mountain air. During their conversation Jesus asked, "Who do men say that I am?" The disciples responded around the circle, suggesting that some people thought He was John the Baptist. Others thought that He was Elijah. And some people thought He was Jeremiah.

Then Jesus began to focus in on them more intently as He asked, "But who do you say I am?"

It was in response to this question that Peter made that marvelous proclamation, "Thou art the Christ, the Son of the living God."

Jesus must have smiled and nodded toward Peter as He said, "Peter, son of Jonah, flesh and blood has not revealed this to you, but My Father who is in heaven."

Then Jesus said, "Thou art Peter, and upon this rock I will build my church; and the gates of hell shall not prevail against it."

Jesus concluded this conversation by saying, "I will give unto thee the keys of the kingdom of heaven: and whatsoever thou shalt bind on earth shall be bound in heaven: and whatsoever thou shalt loose on earth shall be loosed in heaven."

Any Bible student knows that this paragraph is overflowing with exegetical problems and has been the focus of much debate. But this paragraph contains four ideas that have helped me to understand the Church more fully and to love it more completely.

First of all, the Church's nature is both divine and human. Every Bible student who has ever tried to do an exegesis of the passage knows the problems involved with the phrase, "On this rock I will build my church." This is a play on words. The Greek word for Peter is *Petros,* and the Greek word for rock is *petra.* So Peter, the person, and Peter, the rock, sound very much alike. But Jesus didn't speak Greek. He spoke Aramaic, which has no gender. In Aramaic the word for Peter and the word for rock are identical. The word *cephas* stands for both

Peter, the person, and Peter, the rock. For two centuries the Church debated this issue of Peter, the rock. Was Peter the rock or was his faith in Christ, the Rock? The fact is that both are true, for the Church is both Peter and Jesus, both human and divine.

Here is a story to illustrate the point:

When Jesus returned to heaven from His sojourn on earth, He gave a report to His Heavenly Father. He reported on His great experiences such as walking on the water and healing the sick. He gave an eyewitness account of His last seven days up through the moment He cried out with a loud voice from the Cross and said, "Into thy hands I commend my spirit." According to the story, God the Father smiled and nodded approval at all Jesus had to report. Then the Father said, "Son, You have done well. You have finished all I gave You to do. But I have just one question to ask. What have You done to be sure Your work is going to be carried out on earth now that You are returned to heaven?"

Jesus bowed His head for a thoughtful moment before He lifted His face with a mixed expression of joy and anxiety. "Down on earth," He said, "I have 11 men. They are just ordinary men, most of them fishermen. One of them named Peter was the first person who ever confessed Me as Lord at a place called Caesarea Philippi. On the shoulders of Peter and his friends rests the full responsibility of Christianity. If they fail Me, My death has been in vain."

The story is imaginary, but the truth of it is not. Christ, <u>our risen Lord, needs imperfect people like Peter and us,</u> and we need Him because the nature of the Church is both divine and human.

→ Does He need Us?

The Church is both visible and invisible. When Peter said, "Thou art the Christ, the son of the living God," Jesus replied, "Blessed art thou, Simon Barjona: for flesh and blood hath not revealed it unto thee, but my Father which is in heaven" (Matt. 16:16-17).

I once heard about a Scottish preacher who went into the church house every Saturday night to pray for his congregation. Since every pastor has a mental picture of the congregation on Sunday morning, it was not hard for him to picture his parishioners in their places. So he would stand in the pulpit and pray for the families, row by row, beginning with one side and then the other. Finally, after he had prayed for everyone, he would walk down the center aisle and stop at the back, turn toward the pulpit, and pray for the man who would preach from it the next morning.

This idea struck me as very useful. So I prayed for my congregation in this manner many times. But when I came to some families, my praying would hit a snag. I remember one elderly man in my church who seemed to get his kicks from thinking up mean things to say to me. Nothing I said or did met with his approval. And he seemed to make his most harsh comments in the presence of others. People like him are a part of the visible church you cannot ignore. And it is with the visible church we have our troubles.

But alongside the visible church is the invisible Church. John caught a glimpse of the Church you cannot see without heavenly vision. He said, "I saw a great white throne, and him that sat on it, from whose face the earth and the heaven fled away; and there was found no place for them. And I saw the dead, small and great, stand before God; and the books were opened: and another book was opened, which is the book of life: and the dead were judged out of those things which were written in the books, according to their works. And the sea gave up the dead which were in it; and death and hell delivered up the dead which were in them: and they were judged every man according to their works. And death and hell were cast into the lake of fire. This is the second death. And whosoever was not found written in the book of life was cast into the lake of fire" (Rev. 20:11-15).

When our Lord returns to the earth, membership in the visible church will not guarantee final salvation. The redeemed are those whose names are on the roll of the invisible Church as listed in the book of life. That is why Jesus warned us against trying to separate the tares from the wheat. Only God knows who belongs to the invisible Church.

The Church is both weak and strong. Jesus said of His Church, "The gates of hell shall not prevail against it" (Matt. 16:18). The gates of hell must be barricaded and guarded from within like the Berlin Wall to keep people from escaping. But they cannot withstand the power of the Church. The Church has rescued many souls from the jaws of death and hell. Yet the Church is made up of weak people like you and me.

More than 30 years ago, Paul Tournier, the Christian psychiatrist from Switzerland, wrote a book *The Weak and the Strong.* The entire book is built around the idea that weakness and strength are just different responses to the same fear. Two people see blood. One faints and the other rises to the occasion and saves someone's life. We call the one weak who faced his fear by fainting and the other one strong who faced his fear by rising to the need. However, the person who was weak at the sight of blood may be strong in another setting. And the person who was strong at the sight of blood may be weak in facing a different circumstance. This is the way the Church is. Both the visible and the invisible Church are made up of people who are weak in the face of many fears and totally invincible in the face of others.

I know of a little church that only had 12 members. And one of those committed suicide, which is enough to bring havoc into much larger congregations. There were three men who constituted a power bloc in that church, dominating all the decision-making process. Their names were Peter, James, and John.

They had two men in their church who were known as the Sons of Thunder. I've had some of their relatives in places where I have pastored. If the Sons of Thunder were present, you can be sure that the old man Thunder himself was not far away. He is the person who taught his sons to yell and argue in their fishing boats until the sound seemed like thunder rolling off the water.

They had one negative member known by insiders as doubting Thomas. Once when the Lord appeared to the little church during a Sunday night service, Thomas was absent. When the others tried to tell him about the visitation, he wouldn't believe it. Not until the next Sunday night when Christ came again would he fall to his knees and cry, "My Lord and my God" (John 20:28).

That little congregation had every reason to be at each other's throats and to destroy themselves as a church. One quality held them together: They were invincible in the power of Christ. They demonstrated again and again that Christ will build His church, and the gates of hell shall not prevail against it. They stunned the thundering legions of the Roman army who couldn't cope with these fearless men and the invincible power behind them. They perplexed emperors who thought this religious sect was only a nuisance and could be stopped by persecution. They met head-on with the mystery religions from the East and the philosophers from Greece. And in the fourth century, they silenced the opposition as Constantine made Christianity the official religion of the Roman Empire. Let us never forget that the Church is both weak and strong.

The Church is in this world and in the world to come. Jesus said, "And I will give unto thee the keys of the kingdom of heaven: and whatsoever thou shalt bind on earth shall be bound in heaven: and whatsoever thou shalt loose on earth shall be loosed in heaven" (Matt. 16:19).

Any view of the Church that is confined to the visible church is woefully lacking. Christ's view of the Church included real flesh-and-blood people here on earth who would become the Church triumphant in the world to come. Every believer in Christ is part of a Church that was, the Church that is, and the Church that is becoming.

When Paul stood on the threshold between life and death, he looked in three directions. *First, he turned back to reflect on his life* and said, "For I am now ready to be offered, and the time of my departure is at hand. I have fought a good fight, I have finished my course, I have kept the faith" (2 Tim. 4:6-7).

It is wonderful to live until you feel you have finished your work on earth. At age 78, Mahatma Gandhi was talking to his followers about the kinds of diet and living habits that would make it possible for him to live 125 years. He said that much time was needed for him to complete his work. But within days, Gandhi was cut down by three assassin's bullets at close range, and he did not get to finish his lifework.

At 91, my mother died without any disease or stroke. Her body just wore out. Not long before she died, she told me her mind said that her life was finished. She wanted to go to heaven. But she said to me, "My body just won't cooperate." Apparently Paul felt he had finished his work on earth, and he was ready to go. "I am now ready to be offered, and the time of my departure is at hand" (2 Tim. 4:6).

Then he said, "I have fought a good fight . . . I have kept the faith" (v. 7). No one can deny that life is a fight. But not everyone who fights hard in life keeps his faith. There were times when Paul must have felt as if God had forgotten him. In Lystra he was left on a pile of stones to die, and in Rome he was kept in a windowless dungeon. Paul could have lost faith in people. Barnabas broke off their partnership and took his nephew, John Mark, to establish their own missionary enterprise. Paul said of one of his friends, "Demas hath forsaken me, having loved this present world" (v. 10). And of another he said, "Alexander the coppersmith did me much evil" (v. 14). But through it all, Paul kept the faith.

Second, Paul turned away from life as it had been and looked beyond death to see life as it would be. "Henceforth there is laid up for me a crown of righteousness, which the Lord, the righteous judge, shall give me at that day" (2 Tim. 4:8).

Paul knew what it was like to stand before an unrighteous judge whose decisions were controlled by his own self-interest. He had seen the laurel wreaths given to men who won athletic events and crowns of gold given to heads of state.

But he also knew that the laurel wreath withered and the crown of gold was always passed, in due time, to another. That is why he looked forward to a judge who would give him a crown of righteousness that he would wear for ever and ever.

Next, Paul turned his eyes and heart toward you and me as he said, "And not to me only, but unto all them also that love his appearing" (2 Tim. 4:8). Christ did not build a church only for Paul and his generation. He built a church with eternal consequences. He built a church for us.

* * *

During the last decade of the 19th century, there was a great revival of holiness that began to burn in many places across the United States. It started in southern California with a little man in his 50s who had been a Methodist pastor, district superintendent, and chairman of the board of the University of Southern California. To help conserve the results of this revival and to keep the flames going, Dr. Phineas F. Bresee gave up the status and security of his place in Methodism and began what would become a new denomination. He moved the physical location of the revival to a hastily constructed building near downtown Los Angeles, a place the people soon called the Glory Barn.

Only 82 people signed the original charter of the Church of the Nazarene. But they were a spiritual movement on their way. The first piece of promotional literature ever printed by the Church of the Nazarene said, "It is not a mission but a church with a mission. . . . Its mission is to everyone upon whom the battle of life has been sore, and to every heart that hungers for cleansing from sin."

After three years of this kind of revival spirit, the crowds were coming. Dr. Bresee wrote about this new, growing congregation: "The poorest of the poor are entitled to a front seat at the Church of the Nazarene, the only condition being that they come early enough to get one."

That revival swept across Texas where men like Bud Robinson, J. B. Chapman, and R. T. Williams became a part of it. It swept across the southland and centered in Nashville, where a Presbyterian preacher by the name of J. O. McClurkan became a fiery spiritual leader.

The revival kept on moving, connecting groups in New York and New England who were experiencing similar fires of revival. Back in the Midwest a flaming spiritual church was organized in Chicago. That congregation took in more than 400 new members in its first year. And every one of us, in one way or another, is a benefactor of that revival, which resulted in the Church of the Nazarene at Pilot Point, Tex., in 1908.

We are not only part of the church that was but also part of a church that is. I wish I could put everyone on a great elevator that would take us into the sky far enough to see the Church of the Nazarene around the world. I wish we could see our headquarters in Kansas City, our seminary, and our publishing house. I wish we could look down on the eight liberal arts colleges of the Church of the Nazarene in the United States with approximately 11,000 students enrolled plus additional schools in many world areas. I wish we could look down on the International Church of the Nazarene around the world with churches in North America, England, Europe, Africa, Asia, New Zealand, Australia, India, and even an underground church in China. When you and I pray a prayer or give a dollar, it does not stop in our local church, for we are full partners with all the other Nazarene congregations great and small. We are part of a church that is.

We are also part of a church that is becoming. My father was part of the church that was. He was a first-generation Nazarene who closed his last revival on Sunday and went into the hospital on Tuesday where he died at age 84. Many of you join me in feeling the responsibility for carrying the baton we have received from those who ran the race before us. But one day we, too, shall lay down our work, which will be picked up by our sons and daughters—the church that is becoming.

One day the Lord will have finished building His Church. The signal will be given that enough is enough. The trumpets will sound. The dead in Christ shall rise, and those who are alive will be caught up to meet them in the air.

I don't know where heaven is, but I can tell you where I hope it is. I hope it will be right here on earth. If there were no more sin, heartache, suffering, misunderstanding, or separation, wouldn't this be a great place to live forever? In our glorified bodies we could gather in our church to *sing* as we've never sung before, and *praise* Him as we've never praised Him before, and *love* Him as we have never loved Him before. But wherever heaven is, there is one hymn we'll sing with new appreciation:

> *The Church's one Foundation*
>   *Is Jesus Christ, her Lord.*
> *She is His new creation*
>   *By water and the word.*
> *From heav'n He came and sought her*
>   *To be His holy bride;*
> *With His own blood He bought her,*
>   *And for her life He died.*

I love the Church, and from time to time I pledge myself anew to its purposes. It is the source of my greatest fulfillment and, at the same time, the source of my greatest frustrations. But I'm committed to it just the same. And I believe I more easily accept the nature of the Church when I understand these facts about it: (1) The Church is both human and divine, (2) the Church is both visible and invisible, (3) the Church is both weak and strong, and (4) the Church is of this world and of the world to come.

The purpose of this chapter:
To examine the nature of the Church that provides room for both fulfillment and frustration among the fellowship of believers.

QUESTIONS FOR THOUGHT AND DISCUSSION

1. To whom did Jesus make His proclamation about building the Church? Where? And why them?
2. How is it that someone or some organization can be the source of your greatest frustration and your greatest fulfillment?
3. In what ways is the Church both human and divine?
4. How is the Church visible and not visible?
5. In what ways is your church both weak and strong?
6. What were the three directions Paul looked from his prison cell in Rome?

Chapter **4**

Entering the Kingdom and Joining the Church

Scriptural Stepping-stones

From that time . . .
> Jesus began to preach, and to say, Repent: for *the kingdom of heaven is at hand.*
>
> Matt. 4:17

* * *

And Jesus . . .
> went about all Galilee, teaching in their synagogues, and preaching *the gospel of the kingdom,* and healing all manner of sickness and all manner of disease among the people.
>
> Matt. 4:23

* * *

For I say . . .
> unto you, That except your righteousness shall exceed the righteousness of the scribes and Pharisees, ye shall in no case *enter into the kingdom of heaven.*
>
> Matt. 5:20

Thy kingdom come. . . .
   Thy will be done in earth, as it is in heaven.
                                        Matt. 6:10

                    * * *

But *seek ye first* . . .
   the kingdom of God, and his righteousness; and all these things shall be added unto you.
                                        Matt. 6:33

                    * * *

Not every one . . .
   that saith unto me, Lord, Lord, shall enter into the kingdom of heaven; but he that doeth the will of my Father which is in heaven.
                                        Matt. 7:21

                    * * *

Clare Boothe Luce came to Boston for a speech in which she said, "Every man's life can be reduced to just one sentence."

She explained that the life of Dwight Eisenhower could be capsulized in the statement, "He was the commander in chief of the Allied forces during the conquest of Europe." Everything Eisenhower did before the invasion, she said, was preparation for the fulfillment of his life on the beaches of Normandy and in the fall of Berlin. And everything Eisenhower did after the war, including the presidency of Columbia

University and being president of the United States, was an anticlimax.

Mrs. Luce said the life of Abraham Lincoln could be summarized in the sentence, "He signed the Emancipation Proclamation that freed the slaves." It had been a long time since young Abe Lincoln stood before an auctioneer's stand in New Orleans to see the selling of a beautiful mulatto girl to a lascivious-looking Frenchman. It had been a long time since he had said, "Someday I'll hit that thing, and when I do, I'll hit it hard." But the few strokes of a pen that placed his signature on the Emancipation Proclamation symbolized everything Mr. Lincoln stood for.

Had it not been for Watergate, Mrs. Luce said, the life of Richard Nixon could be described in the sentence, "He opened up China again to the Western world."

Not only can a man's life be reduced to one sentence, but the preaching of most ministers can be reduced to one theme.

The titles Billy Graham gives to his sermons really don't matter. He always preaches on sin and repentance. Last New Year's Eve I listened to his sermon televised from Williamsburg, Va. Before he began, someone asked me what I thought Billy Graham would preach about on New Year's Eve in Williamsburg. I predicted accurately when I said he would begin talking about Williamsburg, and as soon as he had that out of the way, he would preach on sin and repentance.

In 1946, Mrs. Parrott and I made a trip to New York. On Sunday night we attended the Marble Collegiate Church on Fifth Avenue. Although we arrived on time, the ushers had difficulty locating seats for us. We had to be seated separately in the balcony, as two seats together were not available. That night I heard Norman Vincent Peale preach on the power of positive thinking. Norman Vincent Peale preached thousands of sermons in the Marble Collegiate Church over more than a 50-year span. But he always preached on the same theme—positive thinking.

If Dr. G. B. Williamson were alive, he would preach on Bible holiness. If Paul Martin were alive, he would preach on most anything, but it would turn out to be the joy of serving Jesus. *And if Jesus were here, in the flesh, He would preach to you and me about the kingdom of God.*

Jesus began His preaching in Capernaum in Galilee, and He concluded three years later in Jerusalem. But wherever He preached, His message was always on one single theme: the kingdom of God.

The kingdom of God, used interchangeably with the phrase kingdom of heaven, was mentioned by Jesus 115 times in the Synoptic Gospels. And 209 verses out of a total of 600 are used to tell about the miracles of Jesus, which He saw as signs of the Kingdom.

To present the ministry of Jesus without presenting the kingdom of God is like preaching on Noah without mentioning the Flood, or preaching on Moses without referring to the Exodus. Jesus was the Son of Man, the promised Messiah; and the message He preached was, "God's kingdom is at hand."

To get an idea of the importance of the kingdom of God to the ministry of Jesus, let's take a quick walk through His preaching ministry from the beginning:

Even before Jesus began to preach, His forerunner, John the Baptist, stood on the banks of the Jordan and cried out to the people, "Repent ye: for the *kingdom of heaven* is at hand" (Matt. 3:2).

After John the Baptist was put in jail, Mark reports that "Jesus came into Galilee, preaching *the gospel of the kingdom of God,* and saying, The time is fulfilled, and *the kingdom of God* is at hand: repent ye, and believe the gospel" (1:14-15).

After His baptism, Jesus was led by the Spirit to the top of a high mountain where the devil tempted Him by offering Him the kingdoms of this world. Rejecting the offer of earthly power and territory, Jesus came down the mountain to establish a Kingdom that was not of this world. Matthew says, "From that time Jesus began to preach, and to say, Repent: for *the kingdom of heaven* is at hand" (4:17).

On a very busy Sabbath, Jesus sat at sundown, reflecting on the ministry of the day, which included preaching in the synagogue and healing Peter's mother-in-law. Suddenly He interrupted the disciples' conversation by announcing His intention to tour all the cities of Galilee. He said, "I must preach the *kingdom of God* to other cities also: for therefore am I sent" (Luke 4:43).

When Jesus was asked when the end of the world would come, He said, "And this gospel of *the kingdom* shall be preached in all the world for a witness unto all nations; and then shall the end come" (Matt. 24:14).

Finally, we come to the end of Jesus' ministry during the 40 days following the Resurrection. The Book of Acts says the purpose of this time was to certify the Resurrection by "many infallible proofs" and to teach to the disciples "the things pertaining to *the kingdom of God"* (1:3).

The best single compendium of Jesus' teaching on the kingdom of God is contained in the Sermon on the Mount. It opens with the eight Beatitudes, which are guidelines to life in the Kingdom. The first and last beatitudes refer directly to the Kingdom: "Blessed are the poor in spirit: for theirs is the kingdom of heaven"; and, "Blessed are they which are persecuted for righteousness' sake: for theirs is the kingdom of heaven" (Matt. 5:3, 10). The sermon ends with strong warnings about people trying to enter the Kingdom through the broad way instead of the narrow way, and against people trying to live in the Kingdom in houses built on sand instead of rock.

In the Sermon on the Mount, Jesus gave three words of instruction concerning the Kingdom that are especially important to us. They are short, plain words, easily understood and easily remembered. The first word is *pray*. Jesus wants you and me to pray for the kingdom of God to rule and reign in our lives. When Jesus taught His disciples to pray, He started by teaching them to pray for the Kingdom: "Thy kingdom come. Thy will be done" (Matt. 6:10). The second word is *seek*. Jesus wants you and me to seek the Kingdom first in our lives. And the third word is *enter*. Jesus wants us to enter the kingdom of God.

Jesus instructed the disciples to pray for the kingdom of God. The disciples were greatly intrigued by the praying of Jesus. The intimate relationship He had with the Heavenly Father came through to them in ways they could not escape. So one day after listening to Him pray, the disciples asked Jesus to instruct them. Perhaps they used some leverage when they reminded Jesus that John had taken time to teach his disciples to pray (Luke 11:1).

Whether the prayer we have in the Sermon on the Mount is an outline of what Jesus taught those disciples to say or is the full prayer, does not really matter. There are four petitions in this prayer (Matt. 6:9-13). The first one is *"Thy kingdom come.* Thy will be done in earth, as it is in heaven."

Jesus also instructed His disciples to (2) pray for their daily bread, (3) pray for the forgiveness of their sins, and (4) pray that they not be led into temptation. But it is significant that the very first petition Jesus taught His disciples to pray was for the coming of God's kingdom in their lives (Matt. 6:10).

Although Jesus' preaching theme was the kingdom of God, He does not define it for the disciples. This indicates they had no doubt as to the meaning of the word *kingdom.* So when Jesus prayed for the kingdom of God to come, the disciples knew what He was talking about.

The disciples knew that Israel had reached the zenith of its glory under King David. After the death of David, the kingdom began to disintegrate. First there was bickering and fighting over succession to the throne. Then the kingdom was divided into two kingdoms. The Northern Kingdom was obliterated by the Syrians and lost forever. Finally, the two tribes that made up the Southern Kingdom were defeated and marched away into 70 years of Babylonian captivity. Long before Jeremiah finished his lamentations and wandered off toward Egypt, prophets such as Isaiah had already written about a suffering servant by whose stripes there would be healing. Ezekiel later wrote about the Son of Man who would appear as God's person to restore Israel.

In the intervening centuries things only got worse. Pompey captured Jerusalem in 62 B.C., and from then on the children of Israel lived under the totalitarian heel of puppet governors appointed by Rome.

Like their ancestors, these disciples were part of a nation that had been reduced to living on political husks. They knew what it was like for the Roman soldiers to take over their homes and use them as their own. Only under fear of death did they walk a mile with a Roman soldier to carry his burden. They hated to pay their taxes to the mother country across the Mediterranean and had long discussions about how a successful revolt could be launched against Rome.

But through the worst of times these Jews never forgot their dream. They were waiting for the Messiah, the messenger of God who would come to restore Israel to the glory she had known under King David. Much of the popularity of Jesus came from the Jewish hope that He was the Messiah who would marshal the peasants and drive the Romans out of Palestine and into the Mediterranean Sea.

The problem Jesus faced in preaching and praying was a Jewish misunderstanding about the nature of His kingdom. Jesus said, "My kingdom is not of this world" (John 18:36). It was obvious He did not want to get involved in the politics of revolution. He said, "Render therefore unto Caesar the things which are Caesar's; and unto God the things that are God's" (Matt. 22:21).

The last time Jesus met with His disciples they were still pushing for a revolution. Standing with Him on the crest of the Mount of Olives just before His ascension, they said, "Lord, wilt thou at this time restore again the kingdom to Israel?" (Acts 1:6). It is obvious they were thinking about a political kingdom with geographical boundaries, armies to defend its borders, and ambassadors to represent the king and the prime minister. This is why the mother of James and John had come privately to Jesus seeking favored jobs for her sons in the new kingdom (Matt. 20:20-21).

It is a strange contradiction that Pilate decided to crucify Jesus because he was afraid of the threat of an earthly kingdom that might be set up in opposition to Rome. At the same time, the Jews were calling for the crucifixion because Jesus had refused to set up the very kingdom Pilate feared.

As we pray today for God's kingdom to come, let's be sure we know what that Kingdom is. God's kingdom is not political. And *God's kingdom is not the Church.* This is why Jesus told the scribes and Pharisees that tax collectors and harlots would go into the Kingdom ahead of them. *The kingdom of God reigns in the lives of persons who have accepted the will of God as the dominating presence in their lives.* The kingdom of God is in you and among you when the will of God rules your life and relationships. This is why Jesus taught His disciples to pray, "Thy kingdom come. Thy will be done in earth, as it is in heaven." Christ is the living presence of God who may be received as Lord of our lives. The kingdom of God is Christ. His presence in our lives brings us under the leadership of His Spirit. Obedience is the hallmark of people in His kingdom.

* * *

Not only did Jesus instruct His disciples to pray for the coming of the Kingdom, but He also *instructed them to seek the kingdom of God first in their lives.*

After He told the disciples to pray for the kingdom of God, Jesus began a long passage in the Sermon on the Mount teaching about things that give many people their worst hang-ups. There are four areas Jesus identified that concern every one of us: money, stature, clothes, and food.

Jesus talked about (1) the folly of trying to lay up *treasures* on earth, "where moth and rust doth corrupt, and where thieves break through and steal" (Matt. 6:19-20). Jesus declared that (2) many of those present were preoccupied with their *stature*. "Which of you by taking thought can add one cubit unto his stature?" (v. 27). Now he might have been talking about physical height, or he could have been taking about status, for both appearance and social stature were very important to the disciples. Then Jesus went on to say (3) there were those among the disciples who were concerned too much over the *clothes* they could afford. "Consider the lilies of the field, how they grow" (vv. 28-30). And finally, Jesus said (4) there were those who spent far too much time and energy worrying over the *food* they ate (vv. 25, 31).

But Jesus' response to all of these hang-ups people have was that none of them demanded a disproportionate amount of time and concern. He said, "Therefore take no thought, saying, What shall we eat? What shall we drink? or, Wherewithal shall we be clothed? (For after all these things do the Gentiles seek:) for your heavenly Father knoweth that ye have need of all these things" (Matt. 6:31-32). Instead of getting preoccupied over all the wrong things, Jesus said, "Seek ye first *the kingdom of God,*" and then all these things like money, status, clothes, and food will come according to your needs (v. 33).

This is the principle of serendipity, which comes from an ancient myth about the king of Serendip who sent his sons to be trained for leadership in his realm. Their wise old teacher took them on a long journey, which was filled with a succession of lessons they needed to learn. However, while they were trying to learn one thing, they learned many other things they hadn't counted on. While working to solve one problem, they solved other problems. While working to reach one goal, they reached many other goals. Jesus here is saying that persons who seek the kingdom of God and His righteousness will find that everything else in life tends to fit into place.

The same principle is true about miracles. Jesus was not a wonder worker, nor was He interested in trying to perform mighty acts to impress people. More often than not, He completed His miracles and then swore the people to secrecy and warned them strongly against telling others about what had happened. The miracles of Jesus were not signs and wonders to impress the people or to prove His relationship with the Father, or even His fullness of the Spirit. They were signs of the kingdom of God. In the life of the person who seeks first the Kingdom, there are always those positive happenings that cannot be explained by cause and effect. These are the miracles of life in the Kingdom.

Jesus taught that it is not possible to place too high a priority on the Kingdom. He explained this many times in His parables. Jesus said that the kingdom of God is like a man who had discovered *a great treasure in a field* (Matt. 13:44). All his life this man had wanted to strike oil or discover a gold mine or find uranium under his garage. Then one day he found a field where a great treasure was held, and no one knew anything about it. What did he do? He went home to sell everything else he had and put every resource together so that he could buy the field. Jesus said this is just how important the kingdom of God is, and this is why every person should seek it first in his life.

Jesus also compared the kingdom of God to a *pearl of great price* (Matt. 13:45-46). He described a buyer of precious stones who had made a career trading valuables. But at one point in his life he suddenly found a pearl that was larger and more beautiful and more exquisite than all the other pearls he had ever seen in the world. Because he had a great appreciation for the quality and value of this precious stone, the man went home to sell all his other pearls, just to buy this one that was more valuable than the rest. Jesus said this is the way it is with the kingdom of God. Get rid of your concern over raiment and food and drink and status. Get rid of your deep concern over how much money you can accumulate. Put God uppermost in your life. When He is first, all of the other things will fall into their rightful places.

Jesus made some very radical statements about the Kingdom just because He believed it should be first in our lives. If a man cannot keep his hands out of some evil business like stealing or murdering, he should have *a hand cut off.* It is better for a man to enter the kingdom of God with only one hand than to miss the Kingdom with both (Matt. 5:30). Or, He said the man who has two eyes that cannot be kept to his own affairs was better off to enter the kingdom of God with only one eye (or maybe even blind) than to miss the Kingdom with both eyes (vv. 28-29).

It is difficult to exaggerate the importance Jesus placed on seeking the kingdom of God ahead of anything else. He said it was *more important than father or mother.* In fact, he said a man should leave his father and mother in order to seek the kingdom of God (Matt. 10:35, 37). He said, "Let the dead bury their dead"; only come and "follow me" (8:22). If you want a fulfilled life, begin first by seeking His kingdom.

* * *

Then Jesus gave a third directive to His disciples concerning the kingdom of God. Not only were they to *pray* for the Kingdom, and *seek* the Kingdom, but also they were to *enter* the kingdom of God. He said, "Except your righteousness shall exceed the righteousness of the scribes and Pharisees, ye shall in no case *enter into the kingdom of heaven"* (Matt. 5:20).

First, we enter the kingdom of God through the new birth. To Nicodemus, Jesus said, "Except a man be born again, he cannot see the *kingdom of God"* (John 3:3). This idea was new to Nicodemus, who believed men studied the law and worked hard at keeping it as a prelude to religious blessings. Nicodemus asked, "How can a man be born when he is old? can he enter the second time into his mother's womb, and be born?" (v. 4).

Jesus persisted with him by saying, "Except a man be born of water and of the Spirit, he cannot enter the *kingdom of God"* (v. 5).

There is also a second way to enter the Kingdom. We must enter the kingdom of God now via the new birth, *but we will enter the kingdom of God ultimately at the end of the age.*

Jesus said there was a certain nobleman who went into a far country to receive a kingdom and then to return. Before he left, he gave each of his 10 servants a certain amount of money, called talents in the ancient world. "And it came to pass, that when he was returned, having received the kingdom, then he commanded these servants to be called unto him, to whom he had given the money, that he might know how much every man had gained by trading" (Luke 19:15).

And today you and I hold in our hands the assets God has given us. None of these is to be buried nor hid under a bushel nor simply placed in a bank for safekeeping. God expects us to live with a daring faith that will invest ourselves in all things that will prepare us for Kingdom living now and forever.

Jesus said the kingdom of heaven was like a sower who went forth to sow. (1) Part of his seed fell by the wayside, and the fowls came and devoured them. (2) Other seed fell upon stony places where there was very little earth. The seed quickly sprang up, but because there was no depth of soil, it was scorched and destroyed by the sun. (3) Still other seeds fell among the thorns and were choked and stunted with no opportunity to grow. (4) But some of the seeds fell into good ground and brought forth fruit, some 100-fold, some 60-fold, some 30-fold (Matt. 13:3-8).

I suppose our lives are like the soil on which the seeds of the Kingdom are sown. We all suffer limitations and afflictions. We are all in various stages of growth and development. No one needs to build a case for the imperfections among us. Some seed has fallen on stony ground and has never taken root. Other seed sprang up quickly and was soon scorched and withered by distress and persecution. Other seeds were choked by the thorns of the cares of life that prick us on every side. But in every church and in every Christian life there are seeds that will render 30-, 60-, and 100-fold. "The time is fulfilled, and the *kingdom of God* is at hand: repent ye, and believe the gospel" (Mark 1:15).

The purpose of this chapter:
To show the importance of the Kingdom in the preaching and teaching of Jesus.

QUESTIONS FOR THOUGHT AND DISCUSSION
1. What is the kingdom of God?
2. Why was the idea of the kingdom of God central in the teaching of Jesus?
3. What is the difference between the kingdom of God and the Church?
4. What was the biggest problem Jesus faced in proclaiming the Kingdom to the Jews?
5. In what context did Jesus direct His disciples to pray for the kingdom of God?
6. How do we enter the kingdom of God?

Book Three

HOLINESS EVANGELISM AND HIGHER EDUCATION

*A Point of View
on Book Three:*

> The future church that is effective in serving its community will see evangelization as a process and not an event. If we save souls and not minds, we have not saved the world at all. Christian higher education will continue to be the great conservator of evangelism.

Chapter 5

The Wesley Brothers and Holiness Evangelism

Scriptural Stepping-stones

And when the day . . .

> of Pentecost was fully come, they were *all with one accord in one place.* And suddenly there came a sound from heaven as of a rushing mighty wind, and *it filled all the house* where they were sitting. And there appeared unto them cloven tongues like as of fire, and it sat upon each of them. And *they were all filled with the Holy Ghost,* and began to speak with other tongues, as the Spirit gave them utterance.
>
> Acts 2:1-4

* * *

And there were . . .

> dwelling at Jerusalem Jews, *devout men, out of every nation under heaven.*
>
> Acts 2:5

* * *

Now when this was . . .

> noised abroad, the multitude came together, and were confounded, because that *every man heard them speak in his own language.*
>
> Acts 2:6

In the long, narrow outer room of my office are two very large portraits of John and Charles Wesley. They are on opposite sides of the room, looking out of their gold frames at each other. I love these portraits. I commissioned the artist to paint them for the very places where they hang.

Often I stand between them, looking first at John and then at Charles and back to John again. John is on horseback, holding a Bible in his hand, with the leaves fluttering in the wind. He is dressed in leather riding boots and is wearing a coat designed to protect him from the elements. He rode a quarter of a million miles on horseback and often redeemed the time by reading a book, or even more often, his Bible. I am even more impressed that Mr. Wesley rode in an English saddle. For many American riders it would be tricky business to ride and read at the same time. John was a doer, a proclaimer, a preacher, and an organizer. He was a leader who went where the action was and generated the action where he went. John was the leader of the 18th-century revival that swept England.

In my portraits, Charles has a more serene look in his face than John. His feet are firmly on the ground. He is wearing the beautiful clerical robe typical of his day, and he holds a hymnbook in his hand. Charles tended to stay home while John traveled. He was a poet, a contemplative. Charles was the one responsible for more than 6,000 Methodist hymns. Someone figured that Charles averaged writing more than 3 hymns per week for all of his adult life. He died in his 80s.

When John was in London, Charles rode over to his house on horseback every day. Invariably he composed a hymn as he rode. Charles's habit of composing hymns on horseback was so firmly set that the servant at John's house would watch for his coming and be ready with paper, quill, and ink when he arrived. While the servant put the horse in the stall, Charles would sit and scratch out on paper the hymn he had composed en route. None of the books on Charles Wesley that I know about has a chapter called "Hymns on Horseback." But in some of the Wesley hymns we enjoy the most, we feel the rhythmic lurching of the horse Charles experienced as he composed the hymns.

As I look at those paintings, I am reminded that John is the most famous and is the recognized leader of the great 18th-century revival in England. But when I look at Charles, I say to myself that he was really a very extraordinary person.

To begin with, Charles was the 18th child in a family of 19 children. Many of them had died in childhood; yet can you imagine what it would take to adjust yourself to the dynamics of having many brothers and sisters all older than yourself? (And, I might say, can you imagine how impoverished our hymnbook might have been if the Wesleys had only had 17 children?)

Charles was an extraordinary person also because he adjusted well to having such unusual parents. One of the sad observations I have made is the inability of some sons and daughters to cope with their very successful parents. Some children are so overwhelmed by strong parents that they have no identity beyond the reflected glory of their father or mother. Others respond in an opposite way by rebelling and rejecting the values of their outstanding father or mother. In either case, the children settle for underachievement and never become what they might have been.

Charles had to cope with all the problems of having an outstanding father and an unusually gifted mother. His father was a scholarly man who pastored the church in Epworth for 39 years. He was a writer of books on Old Testament subjects.

And if Charles Wesley's father was unusual, his mother was even more outstanding. Besides bearing 19 children, she personally taught all 10 of the surviving children in her own school setup, a room adjacent to the kitchen, operated for six hours a day, six days a week. All the children were taught to fear the rod and cry softly. At five years of age, each child was expected to learn the entire alphabet perfectly, and from there they began to read. Charles had an older sister who could read anything by the time she was six and could read the New Testament in Greek when she was eight.

There is another reason I see Charles Wesley as a really extraordinary person. This was his *ability to cope with the problems of having an outstanding older brother.* John Wesley was five years old when Charles was born. Not only was John outstanding, but he also experienced a dramatic rescue from a tragic fire that gave him a sense of personal destiny about himself.

Sibling rivalry is a powerful source of conflict among children even in adulthood. It is no accident the prodigal son in the Bible was a younger brother who got tired of the sanctimonious ways and the feelings of superiority in his older brother. Charles Wesley, however, apparently adjusted well to his older brother John, for they had a strong, positive relationship.

Another characteristic of Charles Wesley made him extraordinary. *He had an outstanding record on the campus of Oxford.* Charles attended a preparatory school in London and then enrolled in Oxford just as John was graduating. He took his studies seriously, and while there, developed a group of students around him who were known as the Holy Club. They were committed to self-discipline that involved keeping all the campus rules, attending services regularly, receiving the sacrament, and helping the poor, especially the prisoners. The Holy Club did not fail to catch the attention of the other students on campus, who began to call Charles and his friends "methodists" because they had a system for everything.

It seems as if a person like Charles Wesley would have walked from the graduation line into the waiting arms of the world ready to receive and reward him. But it didn't happen that way. *Charles Wesley left Oxford and entered into an experience that could be called his private Gethsemane.*

After graduation, Charles and his brother John accepted job offers in the overseas colony of Georgia. None of us can ever know how much the quest for adventure dominated their decision to go to Georgia. They spiritualized their purpose as ministering to the Indians whose minds, they assumed, had never been debauched by vain philosophy.

But whatever their underlying purposes, nothing went right. To begin with, they tried to cross the North Atlantic in winter, the stormiest season of the year. The storm that hit the little sailboat where the Wesleys were riding nearly broke it in two. John and Charles were overwhelmed with fear and became demoralized spiritually when they saw a group of Moravians who had no fear at all and spent their time in the storm singing hymns and praising God. Even their children were not afraid.

After nearly four months on the ocean, John and Charles really deserved better than they got when they arrived at Savannah. They found a miserable little settlement of 40 houses with not much to offer two ministerial graduates from Oxford. The Indians were apathetic or disinterested, and the Englishmen and Europeans who made up the population were impossible.

John fell in love with a perfectly lovely young lady, Sophia Hopkey, who also loved him. He should have married her, but he didn't. On the rebound she married a rival of John's; and eight days after the marriage, she went to the church, but John refused to give her the sacrament. This enraged her husband, who put the wheels in motion that drove the Wesleys out of Georgia, Charles first and then John.

Things didn't go much better for Charles after he returned to London. Bedridden with pleurisy, Charles finally began to take seriously the spiritual counsel of the Moravians, who helped him see that the death of Christ was not only for the world in general but also for him specifically. And on Thursday evening, May 21, 1738, he believed for salvation. Charles and his friends prayed that night for Charles's brother John and continued to pray for him over the weekend. On Sunday morning, May 24, John arose early, studied his Bible, and prayed from 5:00 until 7:00. In the afternoon, he went to a service at St. Paul's Cathedral and was particularly moved by the anthem. In the evening he went, somewhat reluctantly, to a group Bible study at Aldersgate. And there, while some anonymous person read from Luther's introduction to Romans, John's "heart was strangely warmed." He and his friends went over to Charles's house where they all rejoiced together.

As might be expected, if you looked at those two portraits in my office, John celebrated his conversion the next day by riding off to Oxford to preach a sermon on "By grace are ye saved through faith." Charles stayed home and wrote a hymn.

One year later on the anniversary of his conversion, Charles wrote another hymn, "O for a thousand tongues to sing / My great Redeemer's praise." And thereafter for the rest of his life, he wrote hymns on the anniversaries of his conversion.

There are reasons why Nazarene preachers quote the Wesleys, and why theologians study their hymns and their theology. If the Church of the Nazarene had patron saints, John and Charles would be our saints, though saints without halos. They were thoroughly human, but they were motivated with a divine mission. In a special way, these men and their message is a very important heritage in the church.

* * *

The Church of England during the Wesleyan revival was in a sad condition. The churches for the most part had ceased to be forceful. Religion was under a cloud. The majority of church members had been smothered by a dense fog of materialism. It is unjustified to say that religion in England was dead. But a moral paralysis had crept over the nation that prevented the gospel from displaying its real power. The fact that John Wesley's sermon calling for the renewal of the spirit of revival at Oxford had divided the campus should be no surprise to church history students who have studied the era. It was a time of spiritual and moral apathy.

In 1736, just two years before Wesley's Aldersgate experience, Bishop Joseph Butler wrote the following in the preface to the anthology of religion. "It is come, I know not how, to be taken for granted, by many persons, that Christianity is not so much a subject of inquiry; but that it is now at length, discovered to be fictitious. And accordingly, they treat it as if, in the present age, this were an agreed point among all people of discernment; and nothing remained but to set it up as a principal subject of mirth and ridicule, as it were by way of reprisals, for its having so long interrupted the pleasures of the world."

Another British bishop, George Berkeley, declared in a book written in 1738 that morality and religion in Britain had collapsed "to a degree that has never been known in any Christian country." The prospect, he continued, is "very terrible, and the symptoms grow worse from day to day."

Thomas Seeker, bishop of Oxford, in the very place where Wesley had called for renewal, wrote, "In this we cannot be mistaken, that an open and professed disregard of religion is become, through a variety of unhappy causes, the distinguishing character of the age. . . . Christianity is ridiculed and railed at with very little reserve; and the teachers of it without any at all."

John Wesley had been ineffectual against this background of a powerless church and a materialistic society. If Wesley had died before his 36th birthday, a full year after Aldersgate, his name would not have rated a footnote in history. He was defeated by the fiasco of his own missionary venture to Georgia. He had been leader of religious societies in Oxford, Georgia, and London, with almost no visible or lasting results in any of them. He published a brief theology in 1738, but it did not seem to make any difference to anybody. His book made no ripples. He was a bold critic with a sharp tongue against the established church and the English political system. But he had no instincts for effective change and no power base. As one Wesley biographer, Albert Outler, sees it: "He was an evangelical . . . with next to nothing to show for 36 full years of high-minded diligence." (For almost all that time Wesley had been an evangelical in creed only, not with any saving experience.)

Yet, in less than 10 years, this little man with the aristocratic air and the autocratic ways stood at the head of an evangelistic movement that visibly changed the spiritual tone of a nation. Wesley bypassed the Church of England to preach in the open air. He shook the foundations of the establishment as he found ways to channel and conserve immense spiritual forces unleashed in the revival. Although Aldersgate had warmed his heart, he did not learn until later how to communicate the gospel in terms people could grasp, nor how to lead men into holiness of heart and life.

It is an oversimplification to say the difference in the ministry of John Wesley was the infilling of the Holy Spirit. What the Spirit did for him personally was revolutionary, but it was only the beginning. He not only communicated to his people but also taught them techniques that, combined with the Spirit, were effective in conserving the spiritual ground they had gained. Although no one can say with absolute certainty what made the difference from ineffective to effective evangelism, there are some clues that have been identified by Dr. Outler.

Wesley combined passion with compassion. Before the revival began, Wesley's attitudes were transformed, shifting from stern abrasiveness to sensitivity. It is not enough to be a hard-line, orthodox man whose passion for souls is reflected in emotional intensity and harsh rhetoric. Beyond passion comes compassion.

Some scholars say it was through the self-humiliating experience of open-air preaching that Wesley moved beyond passion for souls to compassion for persons. When he had preached in Gothic, stained-glass churches, Wesley's main concern had been the delivering of his own soul. But when he began preaching in the fields, he was strangely and newly aware of the people as persons who needed healing for their hurts.

Wesley described his preaching in the fields as follows: "At four in the afternoon I submitted to be more vile, and proclaimed in the highways the glad tidings of salvation, speaking from a little eminence in the ground, joining to the city, to about 3,000 people." The scripture from which he spoke was Luke 4:18-19: "The Spirit of the Lord is upon me, because he hath anointed me to preach the gospel to the poor; he hath sent me to heal the brokenhearted, to preach deliverance to the captives, and recovering of sight to the blind, to set at liberty them that are bruised, to preach the acceptable year of the Lord."

This was not the first time John Wesley had preached the glad tidings of salvation, but Albert Outler says it was probably the first time anybody else had really heard what he was trying to say. This should be a reminder in holiness evangelism that the gospel is not preached until it is heard. And it is not heard until it comes across to people with compassion and understanding.

Loudness, crudeness, flailing, and other expressions of intense concern, taken separately or together, do not constitute the secret of effective evangelism. In Wesley, grace had been translated into graciousness. He preached about 800 sermons a year. Most of these were on less than a dozen favorite texts, all of which were intended to expound what J. Glenn Gould caught in the title of his little book on Wesley, *Healing the Hurt of Man.*

Another factor in the spirit of revival for Wesley was his firm conviction that *preaching the new birth is never more than the bare threshold of authentic, fulfilling evangelism.* Being converted was the beginning, not the end. Conversion was the rainbow that arched the entrance onto the pathway of a lifelong pilgrimage in Christ. Wesley warned his followers against the saving of souls they did not have time to nurture. If Wesley were working today with the *Four Spiritual Laws* or Dr. Kennedy's Evangelism Explosion, he would not use either of these approaches indiscriminately. He taught his laymen not only to win souls but also to help stabilize young converts by enrolling them in a small group of helpful Christians.

The sanctified life is the goal of all valid evangelistic endeavor, and this implies a lifelong process. If Wesley were alive today, he would not be very excited about hit-and-run personal evangelism unless there were the follow-through of nurture. New converts need the life-sustaining fellowship of a loving congregation where there is instruction, inspiration, and support. Wesley was 200 years ahead of himself with his own small-group movement.

Wesley did not lead his converts to an isolated, individualistic, existential life in Christ. He outlined rules and regulations to serve as guidelines for converts. In part, these guidelines are as follows:

"It is expected of all those who continue in these Societies that they shall continue to evidence their salvation first, *by doing no harm,* such as . . . ; second, *by doing all the good they can,* such as . . . ; and third, *by attending upon all the ordinances of God,* such as . . ." Now, notice the similarity between these statements and the General Rules of the Church of the Nazarene. Concerning those who desire to unite with the church, the *Manual* says, "They shall evidence their commitment to God—FIRST. *By doing that which is enjoined in the Word of God,* which is our Rule of both faith and practice, including . . . SECOND. *By avoiding evil of every kind,* including . . . THIRD. *By abiding in hearty fellowship with the church, not inveighing against but wholly committed* to its doctrines and usages and actively involved in its continuing witness and outreach . . ." (par. 26).

The similarity between the rules of Wesley for membership in his societies and the General Rules in the *Manual* of the Church of the Nazarene is obvious. The big difference is that Wesley expected converts to join and regularly attend one of the small-group meetings where these rules were learned and understood. He all but mandated attendance in these groups. Nurturing the new converts was only another phase in Wesley's evangelism.

Although Wesley was the focal person in the spirit of revival that encompassed England, *the evangelistic mission on the local level was left primarily in the hands of laymen.* Evangelism has always stressed preaching and personal religious experience. But through the lay witnessing program and the societies, Wesley also majored on the visibility of changed lives that were disciplined and redirected.

Wesley traveled 250,000 miles on horseback, wrote or compiled more than 400 books, and preached an average of more than two sermons per day for many years. However, many of the people in England who were touched by the spirit of the revival heard him preach only a few times in person, and thousands of them never heard him at all. It was the Methodist laymen who made the message and the spirit of the revival visible across England. They practiced Christianity on the job. They did not save spiritual matters for the regularly scheduled meetings of the societies. Inside and outside, in the marketplace, and in their homes, Wesley's converts were involved in the redemption of people in an agonized nation. Redeemed men and women began to move into places of responsibility and leadership in the developing industrial society. They were the principal participants in the least disruptive social and spiritual revolution in history. They were a new class of people, broken free from their shackles of servility to sponsor a Christian revolution that saved England from the bloodbath that developed in France.

* * *

No one can turn back the clock to the good old days by repeating the clichés of the former era. The younger generation is turned off by the images of Canaan land, crossing over Jordan, and the grapes of Eshcol. In the last years of the 20th century, people do not think with the same assumptions, priorities, and values that were standard during the first quarter of the century. The old fears and taboos that have been used for hundreds of years in the moral control systems of Western society have been mortally weakened. Psychological anxiety and religious guilt are no longer merged into one feeling.

Modern man works to understand his psychological anxieties, but ignores religious guilt. New systems of social concern in the culture have taken the clout out of the Ten Commandments for secular people.

Guilt in our society is often no more than anxiety over consequences. Only seldom is guilt related to an awareness of God's unrelenting wrath against sin. Repentance comes hard to a self-righteous generation. Our message is never true evangelism until it receives a response from those who live in today's world.

It is doubtful if preaching alone is going to bring the spirit of revival in any church. We need saints without halos to walk among the young, the apathetic, and the avant-garde of this generation, and demonstrate in understandable terms the transforming love of Christ.

Many Sunday morning television ministries have become commercialized to the point of disgrace. Ranting preachers are finding it harder to bolster their crowds. Turning up the sound system a few more decibels won't do the job. It could be that this is the day of the parish minister who can build into his congregation a cadre of totally committed laymen who become the hands and feet of Jesus to bring the spirit of revival in the local church and the community.

The purpose of this chapter:

To introduce the Wesley brothers, John and Charles, and to relate them to our evangelistic heritage.

QUESTIONS FOR THOUGHT AND DISCUSSION

1. What do you know about the home and family where John and Charles Wesley grew up?

2. Where were John and Charles educated?
3. Why was Charles an outstanding person according to this chapter?
4. What is the difference between passion and compassion in evangelism?
5. Where does sanctification fit in the process of evangelism?
6. In what ways is evangelism important in the future of the church?

Chapter **6**

Holiness and the Educated Person

Scriptural Stepping-stones

Thou wilt keep . . .
> him in perfect peace, *whose mind is stayed on thee:* because he trusteth in thee.
>
> Isa. 26:3

* * *

And he answering said, . . .
> *Thou shalt love the Lord thy God* with all thy heart, and with all thy soul, and with all thy strength, and *with all thy mind;* and thy neighbour as thyself.
>
> Luke 10:27

* * *

For this is the covenant . . .
> that I will make with the house of Israel after those days, saith the Lord; *I will put my laws into their mind,* and *write them in their hearts:* and I will be to them a God, and they shall be to me a people.
>
> Heb. 8:10

But I fear, . . .

> lest by any means, as the serpent beguiled Eve through his subtilty, so your minds should be corrupted from the simplicity that is in Christ.
>
> 2 Cor. 11:3

* * *

And be not conformed . . .

> to this world: but *be ye transformed by the renewing of your mind,* that ye may prove what is that good, and acceptable, and perfect, will of God.
>
> Rom. 12:2

* * *

For to be . . .

> *carnally minded is death;* but to be *spiritually minded is life and peace.*
>
> Rom. 8:6

* * *

A friend of mine was present during a Yale University orientation for parents, when a father stood and asked a question that sent a buzz of response across the auditorium. He said he would like to know what his son was supposed to learn, or be able to do, after attending Yale for four years and paying more than $50,000 in tuition. After stumbling about for an answer, the dean finally said that a degree from Yale represented the completion of a major and a total of 120 semester hours. An audible sound of dissatisfaction swept the meeting. The question was pertinent, and the dean had given an inadequate answer.

I am wondering how we might respond if a similar question were asked at graduation time in one of our holiness colleges. We like to talk about revivals, and pray aloud for the recurrence of an Asbury-type awakening of some years ago. We like to talk about student personnel policies that focus on control and the perpetuation of a holiness life-style. We like to talk about saved and sanctified teachers who are good churchmen and well grounded in the theology of holiness. We like to talk about the personal relationship of faculty to students, and we point with justifiable pride to students who arrived on campus in a state of spiritual rebellion and then "came to themselves" in an old-fashioned revival as a result of good Christian modeling and guidance by faculty who care.

All of these characteristics of a holiness college are good and should never be disparaged. But what about the harder question of holiness and the marks of an educated person? Regardless of the good things that happen to a student, such as a new religious experience or finding a compatible marriage partner, the main purpose for going to college is to get an education. Something happens to a person's mind during four years in college. What should that something be in a college of the Church of the Nazarene?

And let me further suggest that people who are looking for a religion of warm fuzzy feelings get very little support from either the Bible or the theology of John Wesley. *It was strong medicine in his day for Wesley to admonish seekers to use their minds.* Wesley said, "We, . . . earnestly exhort all who seek after true religion to use all the reason which God has given them" (*Wesley's Works* 8:13). He also said he would as soon put out his eyes as to lay aside his reason, and he was ready to give up every opinion he could not defend by calm, clear reason. Wesley had little patience with people who depended more on emotion than reason. "Among them that despise and vilify reason, you may always expect to find those enthusiasts who suppose the dreams of their own imagination to be revelations from God. We cannot expect that men of this turn will pay much regard to reason" (6:351).

And, lest there be any misunderstandings about what he meant by reason, Wesley defined it. "It means a faculty of the human soul; that faculty which exerts itself in three ways: (1) by simple apprehension, (2) by judgment, and (3) by discourse. *Simple apprehension* is barely conceiving a thing in the mind . . . *Judgment* is the determining that the things before conceived either agree with or differ from each other. *Discourse* . . . is the motion or progress of the mind from one judgment to another. The faculty of the soul which includes these three operations I here mean by the term *reason*" (6:353).

Reason, Scripture, and experience, these three, became the legs of an anvil on which Wesley hammered out his theology. His rules on the holiness life-style became the hallmarks of early Methodism.

Personal experience cannot ignore reason without being out of balance. To do so is not only irregular but dangerous. The advocacy of Christian perfection without a major focus on an educated, disciplined, open mind is a contradiction. If we save souls and not minds, we have not saved the world at all.

Some of the great thinkers, beginning with Plato, have tried to determine what constitutes an educated mind. John Henry Newman's *Idea of a University* is still widely quoted on the meaning of a liberal education. John Stuart Mill's *Inauguration Address* at the University of St. Andrews began with some words that have become classic when he talked about men being men before they were lawyers or doctors, and therefore they needed a broader body of study than the technical data in their area of specialty. Robert Hutchins and Mortimer Adler tried to encompass the education of the mind in their Great Books curriculum at the University of Chicago. When I was in graduate school, the Harvard Report on *General Education in a Free Society* was, and still is (with revisions), a landmark in the democratic idea of general education.

When Manning Pattillo, as president of Oglethorpe University, came to speak on the occasion of my inauguration as president of Olivet, he spelled out the eight essential skills of the educated person. I am sure I listened to him with more than ordinary concentration, because Dr. Pattillo provoked me to begin a personal pilgrimage toward finding the marks of an educated person for myself.

I assigned this theme for a faculty retreat. And I have read widely and listened intently to anything and everything on the subject. Across these years I have to appreciate five factors as a minimum I am willing to settle for in an educated person. The following are the minimum skills of an educated mind:

1. The ability to enjoy reading at an advanced level
2. The ability to communicate well
3. A concern for clear thinking

4. A grasp for the history of ideas including the scientific method and the scientific attitude
5. A mature encounter with religion

Unfortunately, it is possible to complete a major and earn 120 hours of academic credit at Yale or any other college and still not be educated. This is a tragic fact. A student can piece together a transcript that meets graduation requirements but really reflects a disproportionate number of courses taught at preferable hours by teachers with reputations for generous grading, or subjects that require a minimum of hours outside the classroom in such pursuits as writing research papers and carrying out lab experiments. That kind of student gets a degree but not an education.

Lest you think I have invested all my concern on the student, I want now to complete the teaching/learning equation. Let's consider problems faced by faculty members on a holiness campus.

* * *

One of the *first problems* to be faced in the future church is the teaching/learning process that identifies the *tension between Christian theology and the secular attitude that dominates our culture.* It's not new—the same tension existed in A.D. 30. Something eternal was happening at Golgotha and the tomb, but the crowds shopping in the bazaars of Jerusalem were completely unaware of it. They missed the whole thing. Today the crosses on our college chapels symbolize eternal values that are lost or unknown to throngs of people outside the campus.

The professors experience the tension between theology and secularism in other ways also. What they learned in graduate school is probably unrelated to the theological concerns of the trustees in a holiness college. It is hard to find an academically respectable seminar or convention to attend that recognizes the values of a holiness institution of higher learning. The cloak of academic respectability does not adjust itself well to the claims of the gospel. Paul, a Sanhedrin man, and the first great thinker in the Christian Church, faced this problem when he said, "But we preach Christ crucified, unto the Jews a stumblingblock, and unto the Greeks foolishness" (1 Cor. 1:23).

The problem of giving academic validity to the claims of the gospel is new to each generation of teachers and every crop of freshmen (who in due time become academically sophisticated seniors). Scholarly inquiry into the nature of man and his environment is a high priority in the teaching/learning process. On a holiness campus this inquiry can be a terrifying threat to the status quo. If the claims of the gospel will not stand the test of vigorous scholarship, then the parameters of truth and faith are unclear and confused for both teacher and student.

The professor and the student on the holiness campus must take the calculated risk of committing themselves emotionally and intellectually to a belief that does not bear the stamp of secular academic credibility. The facts of faith as expounded by Paul's gospel are just that—the facts of faith. They cannot be reduced to neat mathematical equations, but this does not make them any less true. Mortimer Adler said he learned during a severe illness that the God whose existence he could prove was not the God whose help he needed. The compassionate, sensitive God of love known by Abraham, Isaac, and Jacob is the One whom a hurting person will more easily accept.

After the professor and the student in the future church have successfully coped with the academic tension between faith and the scientific attitude, or between the hostility of the secular crowd toward the theological inferences of the Cross, they are then faced with a second serious problem. This can, if not resolved, do havoc to their sense of intellectual honesty. They may find themselves having to resist a *tendency on the part of holiness colleges and their constituencies to totally Christianize the curriculum.*

Zealous Christians seem driven to manipulate their data into Christian shape, to transform the liberal arts into Christian arts. Every dean in a holiness college has faced the problem of those who want to make all studies of literature to be literature that has been Christianized. Somewhere in this process is the cry to ban the book and sometimes even to ban the person who recommended the book or even suggested the book for collateral reading. Even in philosophy and religion an endeavor to read Christ into the writings of Plato and to wrench Platonism out of the parables is unfair to both Christ and Plato. Because he tried to mix Plato and Christ, the Reformation-period scholar Erasmus distorted Plato and misunderstood Christ, says Edmund Fuller. The Christian scholar learns to let Christ be Christ and Plato be Plato.

Western civilization is the product of the coalescence of two radically different cultural roots. One of these, the Greco-Roman root, has its origins in the Greek city-states of the sixth century B.C. The Golden Age of Periclean Athens produced

Plato and Aristotle and finally culminated in the magnificent flower of Roman civilization under Augustus.

The other stream of Western civilization is the Judeo-Christian branch that has its origins in the historic Hebrews of the Old Testament and in the life and ministry of Jesus Christ. His impact on the Mediterranean world was so great that the Roman Empire was declared Christian by the Emperor Constantine in the fourth century.

Since the rise of the scientific age in higher education, the liberal arts have ostensibly ignored their Judeo-Christian heritage, giving themselves to the implications of their Greco-Roman roots. The professor on the Christian campus may be helped in his resolve to alleviate this problem if he recalls the words of his Master when He said, "Render therefore unto Caesar the things which be Caesar's, and unto God the things which be God's" (Luke 20:25). Every undergraduate must learn to enter intelligently into the Church's life of faith and at the same time to gain facility in the life of thought, which is proper in the broader, more inclusive, cultural scene.

However, between faith and intellect there is no natural harmony. Indifference on the part of the Christian student concerning the pagan contributions to the Western way of life, or an indifference on the part of the liberal scholar to the contribution of Christianity to Western civilization, are both blind points of view. They demonstrate two opposite but equal brands of academic prejudice.

There is one further problem to face in the education of the future church. This is the *problem of trying to reach from a liberal, creative perspective but from within the confines of a system nurtured on authoritarian instruction.*

To be open-minded rather than provincial, to be receptive to new truth, and eager for fresh perspectives, are some of the qualities of the educated person. However, these qualities are difficult to develop and stay reconciled with a system that has little tolerance for threatening views. A mind formed by constant reiteration is restless and disturbed in the presence of new ideas.

The theologians who look suspiciously across departmental lines at the psychologists whom they see as apostles of an evil Bohemian doctor are no more open than the psychologists who see the theologians as high-class dogmatists who are hopelessly naive on the real nature of man. Rigid attitudes in teaching and learning are inevitably dogmatic, domineering, and divisive.

Jesus taught principles, and even these were not laid down as dogmatically as many of His followers would have wished. Significantly, He taught the people in parables, which are open to private interpretation. Part of their power is the meaning they have within the context of the day in which they are studied and believed.

One of the frustrations of our day is the overload we have in too many overlapping beliefs. The primary tension is not so much between belief and unbelief as among rival beliefs. Holiness higher education cannot be merely the endless catechizing by authoritarian faculty members and the rote memorizing of their students. While using the most creative teaching methods, there must be a learning outlook that is open, alive, vibrant, and sensitive to truth, both old and new. We must always remind ourselves that all truth is God's truth, and enlightened faith does not need to contradict truth. If an unbeliever discovers truth, it is still truth. And the same book that contains truth may also contain error. Higher education cannot produce educated persons by using the methods of medieval scholasticism. The Judeo-Christian tradition stands tall and straight without apology beside the Greco-Roman tradition. But they must stand side by side, equal heirs to the truth.

And, finally, the teacher and the student who are liberated and fulfilled in the future church are *unswerving in love and service to the church.* Faculty are not God's chosen people to critique and reshape the church. They are God's special category of persons chosen to reflect the church at its best. Classroom work rises beyond the profession of teaching to the higher plateau of ministry when the fulfilled teacher sees what can be done for students in the name and for the sake of Jesus Christ. The classroom teacher with a sense of Christian mission is as much God's servant and Christ's minister as any pastor who stands behind a pulpit or missionary who serves in a third world country.

Sound teaching is essential on a holiness college campus, but the teacher himself is even more important. Brilliant teachers who have not resolved their own problems of faith and authority have managed to wreak havoc on Christian campuses, sweeping bright students along in the fray. But excellent teachers, whose love of Christ and His Church is not compromised in the face of intellectual truth, can be like cities set on a hill. They serve as landmarks in the education of the minds of men and women who will shape the future of the church and the world in the next generation.

The purpose of this chapter:

To explain the importance of quality in holiness higher education.

QUESTIONS FOR THOUGHT AND DISCUSSION

1. What does the Bible have to say about the mind?
2. What is your response to the five characteristics of the educated person?
3. What is the difference between formal and informal education?
4. Can you bring to mind the most important teacher you ever knew? What was he like?
5. Why are holiness and higher education closely related?

Book Four

CONTINUING CONCERNS IN THE CHURCH

A Point of View on Book Four:

The future church that is effective in serving its community will learn to cope with the shattering pace of change in the culture that Alvin Toffler calls "future shock." Although there are other issues for the church, there is space here to reflect on three: the continuing threat of science to faith, the separation factor in television and the media, and the ongoing problems in racism. These problems will not go away by ignoring them.

Chapter 7

Future Shock

Scriptural Stepping-stones

And after three months . . .

> *we departed in a ship* of Alexandria, which had wintered in the isle, whose sign was Castor and Pollux. And landing at Syracuse, we tarried there three days.
>
> Acts 28:11-12

* * *

And from thence . . .

> *we fetched a compass,* and came to Rhegium: and after one day the south wind blew, and we came the next day to Puteoli: where we found brethren, and were desired to tarry with them seven days: and so *we went toward Rome.* And from thence, when the brethren heard of us, they came to meet us as far as Appii forum, and The three taverns: whom when Paul saw, he *thanked God, and took courage.*
>
> Acts 28:13-15

* * *

And *when we came . . .*

> *to Rome,* the *centurion delivered the prisoners* to the captain of the guard: but *Paul was suffered to dwell by himself with a soldier that kept him.*
>
> Acts 28:16

Man has survived equatorial summers and antarctic winters. He has survived Dachau and Hiroshima. He has walked on the surface of the moon and reentered earth's gravitational field with a dramatic splashdown. All these accomplishments make it seem as if man's capacity to adapt to his environment is infinite. But any such generalization is reckless.

There are discoverable limits to the amount of change that human beings can absorb. It is possible to submit masses of people, communities, congregations, families, and individual persons to demands of change that they simply cannot tolerate. As Alvin Toffler told us, "We run the high risk of throwing them into the peculiar state of *future shock.*"

Toffler defines future shock "as the distress, both physical and psychological, that arises from an overload of the human organism's physical adaptive systems and its decision-making processes." Different people react to future shock in different ways, but no one is immune. The future church will be forced to face "future shock."

* * *

Dr. Thomas H. Holmes, of the University of Washington School of Medicine, and a young psychiatrist, Richard Rahe, devised an ingenious research tool for measuring how much change an individual has experienced in a given span of time.

Holmes and Rahe began by listing as many probable changes as they could: divorce, marriage, move to a new home—events that affect each person differently. Moreover, some changes carry greater impact than others. A vacation trip, for example, may represent a pleasant break in the routine but doesn't carry the same impact as the birth of a baby.

Each person questioned in the research was asked to rank in order the specific items on the list according to how much impact each had. It turned out that there was widespread agreement among people as to which changes in their lives require major adaptations and which are comparatively unimportant. This agreement about the impact of various life events extends even across nationality and language barriers. The death of a spouse is almost universally regarded as the single most impactive change that can befall a person in the normal course of life.

By studying the amount of change in a person's life, Holmes and Rahe began to predict the influence of change itself on personal health. To find out, the researchers compiled the "Life Change Scores" of literally thousands of individuals and began the laborious task of comparing these with the medical histories of these same individuals. Never before had there been an instrument devised to correlate change and physical health. The result was startling!

In the United States and Japan, among servicemen and civilians, among pregnant women and the families of leukemia victims, among college athletes and retirees, the same striking pattern was present: *Those with high life-change scores were more likely than their fellows to be ill in the following year.*

In every case the correlation between change and illness was evident. (1) It has been established that alterations in lifestyle that require a great deal of adjustment correlate with illness. This is true whether or not these changes are under the individual's own direct control and whether or not he sees them as desirable or undesirable. (2) Furthermore, the higher the degree of life change, the higher the risk that subsequent illness will be severe. (3) So strong is this evidence that it is becoming possible by studying life-change scores to predict levels of illness in various populations.

With adequate research tools in hand, an attempt was made to forecast sickness patterns in a group of 3,000 navy men who were leaving from San Diego on three cruisers for six months in the Pacific. Each crew member was asked to tell what changes had occurred in his life during the year preceding the voyage. Researchers probed for changes in areas like: relationship with superiors, eating and sleeping habits, friendships, recreation, social activities, family relationships, financial conditions, in-laws, the birth of a baby, or death of a loved one. The questionnaire also indicated the number of times each man had moved to a new home, had trouble with the law over traffic tickets, changed jobs, or was awarded a promotion. The smallest details such as taking a vacation or getting a mortgage were included. In short, the questionnaire tried to cover the kind of life changes that are part of normal existence. It did not ask whether a change was regarded as good or bad, simply whether or not it had occurred.

Just before the 3,000 seamen were to return to San Diego from their six-month journey, research teams flew out to join the ships. These teams proceeded to make a detailed survey of the ships' medical records. Which men had been ill? What distress had they reported? How many days had they been confined to sick bay?

When the last computer runs were completed, the linkage between change and illness was nailed down more firmly than ever. Men in the top 10 percent of life-change units turned out to suffer from one-and-a-half to two times as much illness as those in the bottom 10 percent. Also, the higher the life-change score, the more severe the illness was likely to be.

Let's consider how these conclusions affect society and particularly the future church. If radical changes affect physical health, how much more must the impact of change be on mental and spiritual health? This may be a partial explanation for the spreading use of drugs, the rise of mysticism, the recurrent outbreaks of vandalism and undirected violence, and the sick apathy of millions on the secular scene.

In the Church, there probably has never been a time since the early Christians fought with wild beasts in the arenas of Ephesus and Rome that the Body of Christ has been faced with more radical change. No church family is immune.

I made a list of some changes church people have been forced to face that would not have been considered as church problems a generation ago:

(1) With the development of the microchip and the artificial intelligence of the computer, the economy in Western countries and particularly in the United States *has shifted from a manufacturing base to an information base.* This has resulted in good times and bad times simultaneously as massive numbers of people have lost their jobs, homes, or farms. The uneducated person is having a tough time finding work, and the untrained person is relegated to the jobs paying minimum wage.

As these job changes force families to migrate to new areas, neighborhoods change and congregations are forced to move or change the nature of their ministry. These decisions are agonizing and often divide church families. The consequence of struggling to cope with these changes is almost always some kind of spiritual pathology that infects the entire church.

(2) Who would have ever guessed that the permissive society of the '40s and '50s would have developed into *the promiscuous society of the '60s and '70s that gave us the AIDS epidemic of the 1980s.*

To date, secular society is still looking for prevention that does not contravene their personal rights to a promiscuous life-style. We can only work and pray for the world to see the solution to AIDS in the biblical statutes that call for a monogamous life of sexual purity.

Dianne Feinstein, mayor of San Francisco, a city that is second only to New York in the total number of AIDS cases, cut through all the verbiage about "safe sex" and "civil rights" and said in her message to 7,000 people at the AIDS conference in Washington, D.C., that "we can no longer be a promiscuous society." I'm afraid the ideal of sexual purity is still a long way coming. And in the meantime, churches are going to be faced with choosing their attitudes toward AIDS victims even in their own congregations. Besides sexual contact, AIDS may be spread by blood transfusions and infections through openings in the skin. For now, in most churches, AIDS is still a future shock. The day is coming when that won't be so.

(3) Maybe some congregations have become accustomed to divorce and have learned to adapt. But for me, it's hard. I guess I'm a slow learner. I have no problem loving the people who are victimized by divorce, but I can't get over the shock.

In divorces nobody wins. Initially, each of the spouses is relieved at legal separation from the tensions that generated the divorce. But neither spouse is ready for the self-consciousness, uncertainties, loneliness, and other problems that arise after the judge has finished his work. Most divorced people seek a new relationship in an effort to deal with the problem of isolation. This may or may not be an improvement over their first marriage. Divorces tend to run in families; and the first one is always the hardest.

Children never win in a divorce. They are usually left with a parental schizophrenia that is seldom cured by even the most amiable visitation rights. Any sensitive grade school teacher can recite a litany of depressing episodes with children of single-parent homes who are trying to work through the problems of self-identity.

The church with rigid, negative attitudes toward divorced adults and patronizing ways toward children from divorced homes fails to be therapeutic. But the church that ignores the shock of divorced families is compromising the Bible guidelines on both divorce and forgiveness.

(4) The surgeon general and all the scientists and physicians who have supported his strong stand against smoking have reinforced the platform where the Church of the Nazarene has always stood. I only wish they had the courage to do the same thing with alcohol consumption.

To me, the problem is plain: Total abstinence is the answer to smoking tobacco. *But with alcohol we have compromised from insisting on total abstinence to allowing for temperate consumption.* A church leader is quoted as saying, "We have lost the battle on the movies, and we're losing the battle on wine." I don't know if he's right or not. But I do know that alcoholism as a spiritual, social, and physical sickness is a shock that has to be faced among the families in every church.

Of course we have the related problem of drug abuse. Any church with young people in junior and senior high deals with the issue. Likewise a church that has adult members who depend on prescription drugs for sleep and regular relief from tension has the potential for a problem.

Although my list of future shocks—(1) family dislocations because of our economic shift from a manufacturing to an information society, (2) AIDS and the promiscuous culture, (3) divorce and family breakdown, and (4) alcohol and drug abuse—is not exhaustive, it does indicate some of the radical changes in this generation that the church cannot ignore. The church cannot be silent. It must deal boldly with radical changes that society has come to accept as normal.

But there is something we need to learn for ourselves that goes beyond speaking up on the issues of change. We must learn how to be at peace on the inside when our private world is falling in shambles around us.

For this kind of peace, we can go to the Bible. God's Word is an inexhaustible resource of comfort and reassurance for church people learning how to cope with seemingly limitless change. God's therapy is expressed in many ways:

1. *The therapy of His care:* "Surely *he shall deliver thee from the snare of the fowler, and from the noisome pestilence. He shall cover thee with his feathers,* and under his wings shalt thou trust: his trust shall be thy shield and buckler. *Thou shalt not be afraid for the terror by night; nor for the arrow that flieth by day"* (Ps. 91:3-5).

2. *The therapy of a committed life:* "Because he hath set his love upon me, therefore *will I deliver him: I will set him on high,* because he hath known my name. He shall call upon me, and *I will answer him: I will be with him in trouble; I will deliver him, and honour him. With long life will I satisfy him, and shew him my salvation"* (Ps. 91:14-16).

3. *The therapy of God's strength in us:* "God is our refuge and strength, *a very present help in trouble.* Therefore *will not we fear, though the earth be removed,* and though the mountains be carried into the midst of the sea; though the waters thereof roar and be troubled, though *the mountains shake* with the swelling thereof. Selah" (Ps. 46:1-3).

4. *The therapy of quietness in His presence:* "Be still, and *know that I am God:* I will be exalted among the heathen, I will be exalted in the earth. The Lord of hosts is with us; the God of Jacob is our refuge. Selah" (Ps. 46:10-11).

5. *The therapy of openness:* "Come, ye children, hearken unto me: I will teach you the fear of the Lord. What man is he that desireth life, and loveth many days, that he may see good? *Keep thy tongue from evil,* and thy *lips from speaking guile. Depart from evil,* and *do good; seek peace,* and pursue it" (Ps. 34:11-14).

6. *The therapy of His cleansing:* "Let there be no more *bitter resentment or anger, no more shouting or slander,* and *let there be no bad feeling of any kind among you.* Be *kind to each other,* be *compassionate.* Be as *ready to forgive* others as God for Christ's sake has forgiven you" (Eph. 4:31-32, Phillips).

When Jesus said that we were to forgive "seventy times seven," He was thinking not only of our souls but also of saving our bodies from ulcerative colitis, toxic illnesses, high blood pressure, and a score of other diseases that can result from unforgiveness.

Even in the midst of unprecedented change, church people need not be overwhelmed: "If thou wilt diligently hearken to the voice of the Lord thy God . . . I will put none of these diseases upon thee" (Exod. 15:26).

The purpose of this chapter:
To identify areas of change and future shock that the local church must face, ready or not.

QUESTIONS FOR THOUGHT AND DISCUSSION

1. In what ways do excess and overpowering change make us physically ill?
2. In what ways have you seen radical change overwhelm the coping mechanism of a congregation?
3. What has been the fallout of population changes in changing the character and direction of your church?
4. What does the church need to do, if anything, concerning AIDS, alcoholism, and drug abuse?
5. What is the role of the church in helping families sustain their love and commitment to each other?
6. What promises are most helpful to you when times are tough?

Chapter 8

Science and Faith

Scriptural Stepping-stones

Now we have . . .

> received, not the spirit of the world, but the spirit which is of God; that we might *know the things that are freely given to us of God*. Which things also we speak, not in the words which man's wisdom teacheth, but which the Holy Ghost teacheth; *comparing spiritual things with spiritual*.
>
> 1 Cor. 2:12-13

* * *

But *the natural man* . . .

> *receiveth not the things of the Spirit of God: for they are foolishness unto him:* neither can he know them, because they are spiritually discerned.
>
> 1 Cor. 2:14

* * *

But he that is . . .

> spiritual *judgeth all things,* yet he himself is judged of no man.
>
> 1 Cor. 2:15

For *who hath known . . .*
> *the mind of the Lord,* that he may instruct him? *But we have the mind of Christ.*
>
> 1 Cor. 2:16

* * *

Science is important to everyone. Technology has given the world such communication devices as the telephone, radio, and television. It has revolutionized transportation. It has helped people live longer. Science ushered in the industrial revolution and made possible the mass production that has transformed Western nations from agricultural countries to world powers.

In the home, scientific progress has made life easier and more pleasant. Every room in the house is filled with the results of scientific discovery.

In agriculture, science has revolutionized the raising of crops and livestock. In colonial times, about 90 of every 100 Americans lived on farms. Today, only 12 out of every 100 work in agriculture.

In manufacturing, science has enabled workers to move from the home and small shop to the factory. It has provided a style of life for *working people* that was beyond their fondest imagination.

In medicine, science has given man a longer, healthier life. A person born in this generation can expect to live almost 30 years longer than a person born in 1860.

In war, science has produced terrible new weapons. A guided missile carrying a hydrogen bomb can destroy a city of a million or more. The most frightening reality in the world is that science has provided us with the tools to destroy ourselves.

But science also works in peacetime. The same atomic reactor that powers a submarine can propel a merchant ship. Knowledge about the effects of deadly radiation produced by atomic bombs helps cure disease. The same rocket that sends a guided missile through the air can launch an artificial satellite and place instruments in outer space to help man learn more about the universe. Scientific discoveries can either help or hurt—it's our decision.

* * *

What is science? Science covers the field of human knowledge concerned with facts held together by rules or principles. Scientists discover and test these principles by the scientific method, an orderly system of solving problems. Scientists feel that any subject man can study, by using the scientific method and other special rules of thinking, may be called a science.

Scientific study may be divided between pure science and applied science. *Pure science* summarizes and explains facts and principles discovered about the universe and its inhabitants. *Applied science* uses these discoveries to make things that are useful to man. Most people know more about applied science than pure science because we use the achievements of applied science in our daily lives.

How do scientists work? A scientist is interested mainly in predictable events that can happen again and again. By repeating an experiment, a measurement, or an observation, a scientist helps find the cause of an event. If other scientists are to believe what one scientist learns, the experiment must be designed so that they can repeat it any number of times and get the same results.

A large number of related facts may be organized to form a scientific principle. The principles help scientists find additional facts and principles. The new ideas are linked with the old to make science an organized body of knowledge that keeps on expanding.

What is the scientific method? The scientific method is a way of thinking about problems and solving them. The general rules used today were developed by many men across hundreds of years. The plan a scientist uses to check his work has five steps: (1) stating the problem, (2) forming the hypothesis, (3) testing the hypothesis, (4) interpreting the data, and (5) drawing conclusions. The scientific method is not hard to use. Anyone who is curious can use it effectively.

Was there science in biblical times? Science began thousands of years before man learned to write. No one knows who first discovered fire, invented the wheel, developed the bow and arrow, or tired to explain the rising and setting of the sun. But these events rank as major advances in science. They were among man's first attempts to explain and control the things he saw around him. In general, mathematics was the first of the sciences, followed by the physical sciences, the biological sciences, and then the social sciences.

Dating back at least to Noah and the Flood, the Egyptians invented many tools and techniques. They learned some physiology and surgery while embalming their dead. They developed a practical system of geometry to fix property lines, and a system of mathematics. The Egyptians of Moses' time had studied the stars, named the constellations, and developed a calendar.

William Foxwell Albright, the great archaeologist who taught at Johns Hopkins University, tells in his book *From the Stone Age to Christianity* how the people of ancient Babylon had developed the calendar, the system of measurement, and the system of numbers that were in use during the days of Abraham. In an area somewhat related to ancient science, the people of Babylon developed astrology, which was their means of predicting the future by interpreting the different positions of the stars and planets. Because there are at least eight sets of the alphabet that date back to Abraham's time, we can be assured that the stories of the Old Testament were written and not just handed down by word of mouth as some skeptics have said.

Among the ancient people, the Greeks left the largest scientific heritage. Early in the period between the Old and New Testaments, Hippocrates taught that diseases had natural causes and that the body had the power to repair itself. Aristotle, one of the greatest of the Greek philosophers, studied all areas of science. He demonstrated the need for classifying knowledge, and recognized the importance of observation, especially in biology. He developed deductive logic as a means of reaching conclusions. During this same period, between the Old and New Testaments, Thales, Pythagoras, and Euclid perfected geometry. Other Greeks measured the size of the earth with surprising accuracy. They also mapped the stars. They even developed a unified idea of the universe in which they thought the stars, planets, and sun moved around the earth.

The Romans, during the period of Paul and the Early Church, were interested mainly in applied science. They developed advanced techniques of engineering and government. But they did little work in theoretical science. Galen, who was a doctor of medicine in Rome at about the time Paul died, studied anatomy by caring for injured gladiators.

The Bible is not a book of science and was never intended to be. The Bible is God's Word of reconciliation to lost and alienated men. The story of redemption is not told from a scientific point of view. But this does not mean that the Bible is without scientific fact. Whenever the Bible speaks concerning science or other factual areas, it speaks correctly.

Why then are so many Christians afraid of science? William James, the famous Harvard professor, once wrote a book called *The Will to Believe.* Although it is impossible to put God into a test tube, the lack of objective scientific evidence does not cast doubt on His existence. For those who "will to believe," there is ample and unending evidence that God is real. For those who "do not will to believe," the most satisfactory explanation of a universe without a creator is the theory of evolution.

Many conscientious evangelical Christians oppose schools teaching evolution as a fact when it is only a theory. And many well-meaning educators in public schools resent the attempts of Christians to ignore the contributions of science in their desire to defend the idea of God.

The Bible starts off with one assumption, "In the beginning God . . ." Nowhere does the Bible make any attempt to prove the existence of God. The entire Old and New Testaments are based on the assumption that God exists. To accept Him by faith does not eliminate the further recognition of the unending contribution science has made to daily living. Nor, on the other hand, does the acceptance of the scientific method in all of its many applications preclude faith in God and the existence of such things as love, sin, grace, faith, and forgiveness, realities that cannot be contained in test tubes or explained in equations.

The best of science and the best of faith can live together hand in hand. It is the "will to believe" and the will to accept facts wherever they may lead that cement the relationship between men of faith and men of science.

The purpose of this chapter:
To help church members understand the role of science and how faith relates to it.

QUESTIONS FOR THOUGHT AND DISCUSSION
1. What is science?
2. What is the scientific method?
3. What kind of science existed in Bible days?
4. How do science and faith relate to each other?

Chapter 9

Television and Mass Media

Scriptural Stepping-stones

I charge thee therefore . . .

> before God, and the Lord Jesus Christ, who shall judge the quick and the dead at his appearing and his kingdom; Preach the word; *be instant in season, out of season;* reprove, rebuke, exhort with all longsuffering and doctrine.
>
> 2 Tim. 4:1-2

* * *

For the time will come . . .

> when they will not endure sound doctrine; but after their own lusts shall they heap to themselves *teachers, having itching ears;* and *they shall turn away their ears from the truth, and shall be turned unto fables.*
>
> 2 Tim. 4:3-4

* * *

Television has been around in a big way for nearly a half century. Visitors to the World's Fair in 1933 stood before a television camera and were amazed to see their likenesses reproduced on a screen across the room. RCA had a television in their showroom window in New York City in the 1940s. But not until the 1950s did the American people begin their love affair with the electronic box that dominates most living rooms and all public opinion. TV has become the constant companion of the "yuppie" generation born after World War II.

As Gutenburg's printing press brought learning to the masses through the printed page, so television has brought emotional experiences of all levels to the broad base of the population in our modern world. Television has made it possible for the multitudes to feel the emotional impact of an event in ways the printed page could never do.

The television viewer at a football game has a better seat than the coach. When the astronauts landed on the moon, they took millions of viewers with them. People in many lands saw the actual shooting of President John Kennedy's assassin, Lee Harvey Oswald, and the near execution of President Reagan. Every family has the option of choosing to watch wars from around the world as an accompaniment to their evening meal. Instant sex and violence are available at the touch of a button.

* * *

The screen in the living room can be a blessing, or it can be a deterrent to spiritual values and priorities in the future church.

Television separates us from people. In the early days a housewife went to the village well to draw water. Here she saw her friends, shared the laughs and laments of her neighbors, and in general had a personal view of the community and an opportunity for good relationships.

When the great-great-granddaughter of the colonial housewife was blessed with city water, she no longer needed to visit the well. This made life easier but also less interesting. Electricity, home mail delivery, and the telephone made it easier to stay at home. Today the climax of aloneness is found in the multiple television sets found in most homes. Most women have to be self-starters to even get out of the house. And husbands, when they get home, sit in their easy chairs and control the evening by controlling the choice of channels.

In earlier days, a high motivation for attending a concert, ball game, or political rally was the audience itself. Who you saw was at least as interesting and often more important than the event itself.

While watching television, the viewer is set off from people with a new kind of aloneness. The TV viewer can clap, hiss, or shout, but no one else hears except the family in the other room. The sounds from other people in the audience come through the set in the form of canned laughter and hyped applause. Even the athletic events are timed for the commercial breaks.

The island audiences gather nightly around the television, much as cave dwellers gathered around the fire for warmth, safety, and companionship. And now the people with more than one TV have the option of complete privacy, even from those in their own household. No Supreme Court can correct this segregation, no federal commission can police it. Aloneness, isolation, and separation are built into the dynamics of our television society.

Television separates us from the source of events. Back in the early days of radio, the word *broadcast* entered the language with a new meaning. Prior to the 1920s, broadcast meant to sow seeds over a specific area by hand instead of using mechanical drills. With the invention of the radio, broadcast meant to send messages to unidentified people at any and every possible destination. The mystery of the anonymous audience was what made businessmen doubt whether radio would every pay. They believed in the telegraph and the telephone because these instruments delivered a specific message to a particular recipient. But would members of a vast audience listen to the sender's message while doing other things like driving the car or cooking?

In the age of television, members of the unseen audience are isolated in much the same way. Television is a one-way window. The viewer can see whatever is offered but has no legitimate way to interact. This leads to a feeling of isolation from his government, those who collect his taxes, who provide his public services, and who make the crucial decisions of peace and war. His elected representatives can talk and talk; if the viewer wants to respond, about all he can do is write a letter or send a telegram.

Television tends to separate us from the past. Of all the forces that have threatened our sense of history, none has been more potent than TV. It is more powerful than the radio and has outstripped newspapers and magazines. In fact, the desire of Western man for instantaneous, live information, entertainment, news, and religion has made it more and more difficult for the printed page to survive. Many general interest magazines have either gone out of circulation or live under the threat of being discontinued.

Almost everything about TV focuses interest on the here and now—the exciting, inspiring, or catastrophic instantaneous present. And all of this diminishes our sense of unity with the past.

History is a flowing stream. We are held together by its continuities, by people willing to do their jobs faithfully, by the unspoken resoluteness of those who still believe much of what their fathers believed. That makes a dull television program. So the family begins to think of the outside world as though it, too, is a program that should change every half hour.

There is nothing very exciting about 100 people gathering in an ordinary church house when there are glass cathedrals and great auditoriums with huge choirs, professional musicians, and powerful speakers. But the local pastor has continuity with his parishioners, while the electronic church produces one exciting service and then tunes out our lives until time for the next exciting telecast.

Television separates us from reality. As we turn the knobs and push the buttons on our TV, we may wonder what's real and what isn't. Is this program live, or is it taped? Is it merely an imitation or a simulation? Is it a rerun? When, if ever, did it really occur? Is this happening to real people? Is the church service commercial? Is the political speech propaganda? Are sports just big business? Is this commercial honest? With senses that are dulled with overstimulation, eyes that are glazed, and ears that have heard everything, we dare the comedian to make us laugh, the preacher to motivate our wills, or the ball game to be better than the last one.

Television conquered America in less than a generation. No wonder its powers are bewildering and hard to define. It took 500 years for the printing press to dominate learning. Like the printing press, television has delivered on its promise to transform our culture completely.

The great test of television should be whether it can break down the walls it has built to separate us from one another. The endless stream of dreary talk shows must be someone's idea of trying to bridge the gaps. In the meantime, the sense of personal presence, the sense of neighborhood, of visible fellowship, of publicly shared enthusiasm and dismay must be among those who have turned off their sets and have become involved again with each other.

In the meantime, no religious program can be a substitute for going to church. And sending a CARE package to India—which is a good thing to do—is not the same as getting involved in the life and ministry of a missionary in that same country. The arid lands of television viewing must never be a substitute among Christians for an alive interaction with the world of human beings. TV viewing of religious spectaculars must not quench a living faith that takes us out of the house to do something good for somebody else. And television must never be a substitute for the fellowship of a vital, believing congregation.

The purpose of this chapter:

To sound a warning on the continuing possibility of television without guidelines.

QUESTIONS FOR THOUGHT AND DISCUSSION

1. In what ways is television a blessing?
2. Do you feel television is misused or properly used in your home?
3. What personal TV viewing guidelines do you honor?
4. What losses do we incur by watching television?

Chapter *10*

Racism in the Church

Scriptural Stepping-stones

And, behold, . . .
> *a certain lawyer stood up, and tempted him,* saying, Master, what shall I do to *inherit eternal life?* He said unto him, *What is written in the law?* how readest thou? And he answering said, Thou shalt love the Lord thy God with all thy heart, and with all thy soul, and with all thy strength, and with all thy mind; and *thy neighbour as thyself.* And he said unto him, Thou hast answered right: this do, and thou shalt live.
>
> Luke 10:25-28

* * *

Where there is neither . . .
> *Greek nor Jew,* circumcision nor uncircumcision, *Barbarian, Scythian,* bond nor free: *but Christ is all, and in all.*
>
> Col. 3:11

* * *

The future church will need to face up to racism because its ravages are everywhere. Within Western culture, racism has become a crucial problem, separating people into groups and classes according to their recognizable physical characteristics. Because basic rights have been denied some citizens, enmity and strife have exploded, often escalating into violence and rioting.

The problem of racism is not confined to one nation. It is worldwide. It is doubtful if there is a place on earth where the attitude of racial superiority is not expressed in some form. *Any place where there are easily identifiable differences among people, even of the same race, those in the minority seem always to suffer.*

Racism has even made its way into the Christian Church. It not only hides within the fellowship of this body, but at certain times and places has been supported and promoted by various Christian groups. The message of God's reconciliation with man through Jesus Christ has been proclaimed by people who are not reconciled to one another. Therefore, racism is one of the most vicious enemies of man.

* * *

What is racism? Racism is the feeling that one ethnic group is condemned to inferiority by their physical origins and that another group is destined to superiority. *Webster's New Collegiate Dictionary* defines racism as an "assumption of inherent racial superiority or the purity and superiority of certain races, and consequent discrimination based on any such an assumption." Again and again, the distinctions of physical features including color have been interpreted as marks of superiority or inferiority.

What are the roots of racism? Racism often develops because of historical precedent and the conditioned atmosphere in which children are reared. In areas where racism prevails, children often grow up to be prejudiced because of the favored position of parents and other adults. Racial prejudice is not inborn; it is learned. Children who have not been influenced otherwise will, without question or concern, live and play side by side with children of other races.

Promotion of racial prejudices can also be traced to the desire for economic gain. Intellectuals and professional people who are financially secure are the least threatened by minority groups and often become vocal in favor of minorities. Other people whose livelihood may be threatened by an improved status of minority groups are often the most vocal in finding reasons to keep minorities down. Labor unions have been notorious in their exclusion of minorities. We tend to oppose people who threaten our favored way of life.

Finally, racism is often the expression of a sick personality. Since man is always tempted to project his ignorance, trouble, and failure to others, racial prejudice and discrimination are often the outward expressions of inner frustration and fear.

Racism is a worldwide problem. Nowhere in this century has the idea of racial superiority been more explosively and brutally expressed than in parts of Europe under the domination of Adolph Hitler. His rise to power and temporary control of a large part of Europe were built around one theme, the superiority of the Aryan race.

India, with a population more than twice the size of the United States, is a unique phenomenon in human relations. The caste system, which has been bruised but not broken, governs such areas as occupation, social interaction, economic conditions, and religious teaching. In the development of the caste system, the people of India have been matched against one another. This has been done, not according to race, but according to groupings that have been made within the race.

For generations the Japanese were taught that they were a superior people ruled by a divine emperor, and they themselves were of divine origin. The renunciation of this divinely destined position on the part of Japan after World War II did much in resolving the problem of racism within their nation, though the problem still persists among other Oriental people in the Pacific Basin.

The national television news is often dominated by the ongoing problems associated with apartheid in the Republic of South Africa. The problem is easily focused, and the consequences in servitude and violence are dramatically demonstrated, but the solutions are much more obscured.

The people of the United States represent backgrounds from almost every part of the world. But in a land that proposed to provide a way of life where recognition is given to the freedom and equality of all men, one out of seven of its citizens belongs to a minority group and suffers discrimination of one kind or another. Among these minority groups are the Chinese, Japanese, Indians, Mexicans, and Blacks. At certain times and places the Irish, Catholics, Protestants, eastern Europeans, Russians, or people from Appalachia have been isolated and rejected because they were in the minority. There is a new kind of racism in some parts of America where bright young Orientals with a mind to work are a threat to less-productive jobholders.

What guidance does the Bible give on the problem of racism? The Bible teaches that man is the crowning expression of the creative acts of God. It indicates that the blood of the various races is not essentially different. Racial groups have formed because of the operation of certain processes such as mutation, migration, and isolation.

The Bible has sometimes been used to defend racism. The Puritans of New England justified their attitude toward the Indians by comparing themselves to the Israelites when they were commanded to destroy the Canaanites living in the Promised Land. Noah's curse upon Canaan and identification of the descendants of Ham with the Black people have been used to "prove" that God intended the Black man to be subservient. Paul's injunction "Servants, obey . . . your masters" (Col. 3:22) has been applied to the Black man in his relation with the white majority. But a biblical basis for the assumption of racial superiority cannot be established. Examples of racial prejudice, hatred, and acts of discrimination are used in the Bible as demonstrations of the sin of man.

The Bible speaks to the problems of racism when it declares that all people have a common origin. By tracing the origin of all human beings back to an act of God, the Bible clearly emphasizes the oneness of all men. Man was created in the image of God. All men, without distinction, are made to have a fulfilled relationship with God and with each other.

The biblical emphasis on the relationship of man to God reveals a common need as well as a common origin. Man is a sinner and therefore stands under the judgment of God. All men are sinners regardless of wealth, ancestry, position, color, or nationality. The biblical answer to the common problem of evil is the Savior of all men, Jesus Christ.

In days such as these, Christians must take their stand against racism. There is no place for it in the Christian message or in the fellowship of Christian people. We should lead the way in replacing misunderstandings and ignorance with facts and truth about racism. We can support constructive legislation for community, state, and nation. Christians in congregations must give personal testimony in deed as well as in words to prove their love for God and for their fellowman.

The purpose of this chapter:
To focus attention on the continuing problem of racism, even in the church.

QUESTIONS FOR THOUGHT AND DISCUSSION
1. What is racism?
2. In what way is racism a worldwide problem?
3. What does the Bible say about racism?
4. To what degree, if any, is there a problem of racism in your church?
5. What should the church be doing about racism that it is not already doing?

Book Five

THE LOCAL CHURCH IN AN INTERNATIONAL WORLD

A Point of View on Book Five:

The church is local, but the world is international. Therefore, the future church that is effective in serving its community will be alert to the global issues including hunger, human rights, and war. The future church cannot solve any one of these problems by itself. But it is a shame to be the representative of Jesus Christ in the world today and be oblivious to the global issues of just and unjust laws, and the threat of a nuclear winter. The future church will be increasingly called on to stand up and be counted!

Chapter **11**

Dealing with Unjust Laws

Scriptural Stepping-stones

Let every soul *be* . . .

> *subject unto the higher powers.* For there is no power but of God: the powers that be are ordained of God.
>
> Rom. 13:1

* * *

Whosoever therefore resisteth . . .

> the power, resisteth the ordinance of God: and they that resist shall receive to themselves damnation. For rulers are not a terror to good works, but to the evil. *Wilt thou then not be afraid of the power?* do that which is good, and thou shalt have praise of the same: for he is the minister of God to thee for good. But if thou do that which is evil, be afraid; *for he beareth not the sword in vain:* for he is the minister of God, a revenger to execute wrath upon him that doeth evil.
>
> Rom. 13:2-4

* * *

Wherefore ye must needs be subject, . . .

> not only for wrath, but also for conscience sake. For this cause pay ye tribute also: for they are God's ministers, attending continually upon this very thing.
>
> Rom. 13:5-6

Render therefore . . .
> to all their dues: *tribute to whom tribute is due;* custom to whom custom; fear to whom fear; *honour to whom honour.*
>
> Rom. 13:7

* * *

The future church will need to face up to the only two types of laws there are in the world: just and unjust. And the struggle faced by many Christian adults today concerns two matters related to law. *First,* how can a just law be distinguished from an unjust law? And *second,* what kinds of attitudes and behavior patterns can be adopted toward an unjust law?

Christians will be the first to say, Obey the just laws; this is a moral obligation. But Christians with their eyes open and their minds attuned to the great social issues of the world must be aware that there are also unjust laws. Here then are the hard questions: *First,* what makes a law just or unjust? And *second,* who decides which laws are just or unjust?

To begin with, a just law squares with the moral law. Any law that uplifts human personality is a just law. An unjust law is a code that the majority inflicts on the minority without giving the minority a part in enacting it. An unjust law is passed to protect ourselves and keep the helpless segment within the population under control. The unjust law is taxation without representation.

The second major issue is: If a Christian adult has come to the conclusion by virtue of his own conscience that there are unjust laws, the big question is, How can he deal with them?

Socrates, who was not a Christian, practiced civil disobedience, which resulted in the ultimate demand from his peers that he drink the poison cup of hemlock and die. John Bunyan, who was a Christian, practiced civil disobedience that resulted in his jail experience and made it possible for him to write *Pilgrim's Progress.* The early Christians practiced civil disobedience among the Romans and paid their price among the lions and gladiators in the arenas of the empire. Early Bostonians got their names and deeds reported in the history books because of a massive act of civil disobedience called the Boston Tea Party.

There are several options for Christians who believe they have identified unjust laws:

The *first* reaction to injustice, which is repugnant to most Christians, is some form of *radical, violent response.*

Rioting, bombing, murder, and all other acts of destruction against people and property are inconsistent with the Sermon on the Mount and the teachings of Jesus Christ. The Master spoke out not only against murder but also against anger (which is often the emotional motivation for destroying another person). The route of violence is *not* open to concerned Christians looking for ways to deal with injustice.

Second, an arena of action that *is* open to Christians who want to resist unjust laws is the *judicial system of the country.*

It remains to be seen what Christians could achieve in legislation and politics if they were willing to give themselves to the issues. It takes great amounts of energy and time to change a law, but there are groups who have done it. Numerous Christian laymen and ordained clergymen have been elected to political offices in the last few years. And the spiritual counselor to several presidents of the United States has been a Bible-carrying evangelist who preaches repentance and conversion. It seems there is more opportunity now for Christians to involve themselves in the political system than ever before. For many churchgoing adults, the judicial system offers the best opportunity for changing unjust law.

The *third* method for dealing with unjust law is *acquiescence and surrender.*

In this system, Christians adjust themselves to oppression but dismiss the possibility of doing anything about it. In the presence of injustice, Christians may wring their hands, sit on their hands, or use their hands. Far too many choose the combination of alternately wringing their hands and sitting on them.

But for Christians who choose this route of acquiescence, there is a special moral problem because the willingness to do nothing about injustice is actually a way of cooperating with it. Opposing evil is as much a moral obligation as cooperating with good. The uninvolved Christian is seeking a negative peace like the Pax Romana during the era of the Roman Empire, when all minorities were bludgeoned into silent subjection.

A *final* option for Christians who want to fight injustice is *nonviolent resistance.*

This method was popularized in modern history by Mohandas K. Gandhi, the little man from India who used nonviolence in a self-sacrificing way to free his people from the economic exploitation and political domination inflicted upon them by a foreign power. The same concept was transplanted to Montgomery, Ala., by Martin Luther King, Jr. In the civil rights movement nonviolence became a startling and significant force for change. Whether or not this nonviolent approach is right or wrong is not the purpose of this discussion. But for those who advocate nonviolence in dealing with unjust law, here are a few significant points.

First, advocates of nonviolent resistance proclaim *the means must be as pure as the end.* From Machiavelli on down, many advocates of change have believed the end justifies the means. Communism, for instance, says that lying, deceit, or violence are justified if they help to create a classless society. But advocates of nonviolent resistance believe that the end represents the means in process and the ideal in the making. Unless one adheres to this approach, it is easy to allow the means for changing an unjust law to be as violent and as unjust as the law itself.

Second, those who adhere to the philosophy of nonviolence practice *the principle of noninjury.* This means they consistently refuse to inflict injury upon another. This means the protesting person must avoid acts of physical violence. But it also means that he avoids violence of spirit. Verbal abuse is a form of violence that may inflict wounds that resist healing.

Third, those who advocate nonviolent resistance also *believe suffering can be a powerful social force for change.* The philosophy of violence says that suffering can be a powerful social force by inflicting hurt on somebody else. People in the nonviolent movement believe that one can suffer in a creative manner. The most powerful moment in the civil rights campaign of the 1960s in the United States came when water cannons were turned on a nonviolent crowd of marchers in Birmingham, Ala., and dogs were called in and released against children in the streets. The suffering of the marchers in Birmingham was the turning point in the route to the civil rights legislation of 1964.

Fourth, people in the nonviolent movement believe there is within human nature an amazing potential for goodness despite continuing evidence of evil. In spite of the Ku Klux Klan and the residue of hatred they represent, there was a great positive response among both Southerners and Northerners as our nation took the first big steps toward human equality.

One of the most difficult assignments any Christian faces is controlling his attitudes toward those who have a different value system than his own. The Christian who believes in submitting to injustice for the sake of peace finds it difficult to accept those who resist. Those who practice nonviolent resistance or work through the political system to change injustice find it difficult to accept other church people who simply acquiesce.

I am glad Jesus said we are to *love* our neighbor. Christians can learn how to love persons without necessarily liking all of their ways. A high mark of Christian maturity is the ability to separate another person's behavior and attitudes from the person himself, and love him anyhow.

Two widely divergent views have appeared concerning the relationship of Jesus to the great social issues of His day. It is suggested on the one hand that Jesus did not concern himself with social questions at all. And on the other, He has been hailed as the world's greatest social reformer.

For some, Jesus is seen preoccupied with matters of the soul. He taught a mystical piety. He was content to leave material conditions as He found them. He was not concerned with redress for social wrongs. This view has led some Christians in every generation to completely divorce their religion from their social duties. Because of this, Christianity has sometimes appeared to those outside to be indifferent or even hostile to reform.

But even a superficial examination of the gospel records shows that Jesus *was* concerned with social issues. He proclaimed a gospel of brotherhood. He gathered His first followers into a social unit. His miracles are seen as springing from His passionate desire to help men physically as well as spiritually. The position must be abandoned that regards social questions as beyond the interest of Christ's ministry. Equally wrong, however, is the opposite view, which hails Jesus primarily as a social reformer. Liberal churchmen today generally foster the idea that sin will be gone when poverty and ignorance disappear. This was not Christ's approach. He openly declared that changed conditions were futile apart from changed hearts (Matt. 15:19-20).

To help us understand Jesus' attitude toward the relationship between the state and religion, let us look at the passage in Matthew 22 where He discusses tribute money. This is His memorable declaration about Caesar's rights and the rights of God.

Then went the Pharisees,
and took counsel how they might
entangle him in his talk.
And they sent out unto him
their disciples with the Herodians,
saying, Master, we know that thou art true,
and teachest the way of God in truth,
neither carest thou for any man:
for thou regardest not the person of men.
Tell us therefore,
What thinkest thou?
Is it lawful to give tribute unto Caesar, or not?
But Jesus perceived their wickedness,
and said, Why tempt ye me, ye hypocrites?
Shew me the tribute money.
And they brought unto him a penny.
And he saith unto them,
Whose is this image and superscription?
They say unto him, Caesar's.
Then saith he unto them,
*Render therefore unto Caesar
the things which are Caesar's;
and unto God the things that are God's.*
When they had heard these words,
they marvelled, and left him, and went their way.
Matt. 22:15-22

* * *

To begin with, we need to remember that the question about tribute money was put to Jesus as a deliberate trap. "Then went the Pharisees, and took counsel how they might entangle him in his talk." They hoped to drive Him into an obvious inconsistency or contradiction that could be used further to discredit His cause.

"Is it lawful to give tribute unto Caesar, or not?" The trap had been cleverly devised. It seemed that any answer Jesus gave would leave Him on the embarrassing horns of a dilemma. If He answered yes, the chances were that loyal Jews, angry under Roman taxes and reparation burdens, would be finished with Him. On the other hand, if He answered no, He would be open to a charge of sedition and possible Roman arrest. And if He kept silent, the people around would naturally construe His silence to mean that He did not know His own mind and therefore was not a real prophet at all. Even if He asked for a delay to further consider the question, His influence would be hurt.

But Jesus said, "Shew me the tribute money." And when the coin was presented, He asked, "Whose is this image and superscription?" When they answered, "Caesar's," He said, "Render therefore unto Caesar the things which are Caesar's; and unto God the things that are God's." In other words, Jesus was indicating the dual roles of government and religion. Give Caesar what belongs to him, and give God what belongs to Him.

Law and order are precious achievements. Frequently they are not appreciated until a community or a country moves to the edge of terror and chaos. Although all legal systems are imperfect, due process of law is certainly better than the uncontrolled use of power, whether it be vested in the people of the street or in a benevolent dictator. Therefore the individual who resents legal restraints has no moral right to defy the law. But equally obvious is the fact that laws may be unjust and tyrannical. The Nazis made vicious laws designed to destroy entire categories of people and wreck social values and structures. Today we honor courageous men who defied the Nazi government, not for their own advantage but for justice.

The tradition of honorable disobedience of law runs deep in our system of values. Socrates went to his death saying, "Men of Athens, I honor and love you. But I shall obey God rather than you." Peter and his friends in Jerusalem, when commanded to stop preaching, answered, "We must obey God rather than men" (Acts 5:29, RSV).

These are outstanding moments in the history of mankind. But they raise difficult questions. Any malcontent can claim that God is on his side. What happens if each individual sets himself up as the judge of right and wrong, obeying or disobeying the law as he chooses? The result is social chaos.

Men and women of integrity must avoid regarding the law as the absolute good. Neither can they indulge in the exaggerated individualism that breeds contempt for law. There are three kinds of situations that have been used to justify civil disobedience.

Honest disobedience is a method for getting a case into court. The processes of constitutional government provide methods for testing laws in courts. If a person believes that a specific law is itself illegal, that it is unconstitutional, he may deliberately break the law in order to create a test case. The man who challenges the law in this way is not trying to cheat and is not showing disrespect for legal processes. His act may lead the court to strike down an unconstitutional law. The

Supreme Court is designed to deal with test cases, deliberately planned to test the constitutionality of a law.

People may use disobedience to protest a law when it violates their conscience and they see no opportunity to change it. Normally, when one dislikes a law, he should work to repeal it or modify it rather than disobey it. Certainly in a functioning democracy the former method is normally the right one. But if a tyranny or a corrupt bureaucracy makes orderly change impossible, some form of protest may become necessary. This was the background thinking of America's forefathers who issued the cry against taxation without representation.

Henry David Thoreau, protesting the government's acts toward Mexico and the expansion of slavery, refused to pay his poll tax and went to jail. To his disappointment, his friends paid his tax and the jailer turned him out. It is reported that Ralph Waldo Emerson visited Thoreau in jail and said in a shocked voice, "Henry, what are you doing in there?" To this Thoreau answered, "Waldo, what are you doing out there?" Thoreau was not plotting to harm anybody and was committing no violence, trickery, or cheating. Society could see his act, invoke its penalty, and decide whether its laws were just.

A more extreme type of situation may call for a clear-cut defiance of law. The case of a morally intolerable evil has driven people of integrity to conspiracies of disobedience. Thus, in American history, the evil of Negro slavery led men of conscience to help slaves escape via the Underground Railroad. The Nazi persecution of Jews led the best and bravest of men to disobey laws in order to save the lives of others. Here the effort is not to make an open witness that might persuade the society to change. It is a simple, direct act to save persons from vicious laws. In a government of gangsters, an honest man is likely to be a lawbreaker.

Any justification for disobedience to law may be misused or rationalized. People are glad for theories that justify their own privileges and prejudices. No rule, either of absolute obedience or of absolute individualism, will spare us the necessity to weigh the claims of personal integrity against the claims of society in those cases where the two conflict.

Responsibility does not end with the decision to obey or disobey. When laws are just, the valid reasons for disobedience are removed. And in an open society, those who disagree with the laws have the opportunity to work for their modification. A healthy society leans to cultivate respect for law, for the freedom of men under law, and for the right of men to change law.

The purpose of this chapter:

To provoke thought and discussion on how the church is to deal with unjust laws.

QUESTIONS FOR THOUGHT AND DISCUSSION

1. What is the difference between a just and an unjust law?
2. Do you think churchgoers do a good job of keeping the laws that one must?
3. What options do Christians have in dealing with unjust laws?
4. How did Jesus face the laws of the Romans and the Jews?

5. What are the risks and consequences of nonviolent resistance?
6. In what ways is your church involved in helping to change unjust laws?

Chapter **12**

Nuclear Destruction and/or Peace in Our Time

Scriptural Stepping-stones

Blessed is *the nation . . .*
> *whose God is the Lord;* and the people whom he hath chosen for his own inheritance.
>
> Ps. 33:12

* * *

The Lord looketh from heaven; . . .
> he beholdeth all the sons of men. From the place of his habitation he looketh upon all the inhabitants of the earth. He fashioneth their hearts alike; he considereth all their works.
>
> Ps. 33:13-15

* * *

There is no king saved . . .
> *by the multitude of an host: a mighty man is not delivered by much strength. An horse is a vain thing for safety:* neither shall he deliver any by his great strength.
>
> Ps. 33:16-17

There is one more fact the future church will need to face, and that is the idea of the world as one world, not just a conglomerate of separate little private worlds where people can live in isolation. Although the fact has not yet been accepted by many people, this is one world and only one world. Oceans, swamps, mountains, deserts, and other barriers that once made it possible to be an isolationist are now dissolved. Jet engines, intercontinental missiles, and nuclear fallout make isolationism untenable. To deny the concept of one world is about as senseless as to deny that the earth is round.

But even in one world, there are many divisions that make for conflict. Not everyone speaks the same language. Not everyone hears his own language as others hear it. One man's interpretation of what he says is not the same as another interprets him. Not everybody loves everybody else. Personal and national interests vary from country to country. Life-styles and standards of living are found around the world in infinite variety. And from country to country around the world, values and traditions are in conflict.

But in spite of all these differences, Christians cannot ignore our oneness on the earth. Astronauts can circle the globe several times in one day. A hot line provides instant communication between Moscow, Washington, and other major capitals of the world. Violence in remote parts of the world affects our personal taxes, our safety, and our way of life. A dispute between Israel and her Arab neighbors may involve only a few hundred miles of desert territory, but it threatens our national interests, our money, and even the lives of our children. A revolution in Cuba, central Africa, South America, or Southeast Asia may be of fairly small significance geographically, but it has great importance for every other person worldwide. Whether we know each other or not, whether we like each other or not, we face the common alternatives of either learning to live together or facing possible annihilation.

This is a dangerous world! Spread over the entire world today like a low-hanging, dark cloud is the threat of nuclear terror. One plane or one Polaris-armed submarine can release weapons with far more explosive power than the sum of those used by all the armies in World War II. The Soviet Union and the United States together have explosive power equivalent to 10 tons of TNT for every person on earth. Even the "small" tactical weapons now available for battlefield use have twice the power of the blockbusters used in World War II, plus the additional danger of radioactivity.

The future Church Christians must understand the seriousness of world politics. A secretary of defense in the United States has said, "A full-scale nuclear exchange between the United States and the Soviet Union, lasting less than one hour, would kill almost 100 million Americans—the equivalent of over 300 World War IIs. There would be little comfort in knowing that over 100 million Russians would also be killed."

Although the danger of a nuclear holocaust is already present, it is likely to increase. At least five countries now have nuclear weapons, and that number will increase during the next decade. Even more sobering is the thought of nuclear weapons in the hands of terrorists.

Every president since Harry S. Truman has spoken forcefully about the national disaster of nuclear war. President Eisenhower said, "With both sides of this divided world in possession of unbelievably destructive weapons, mankind approaches a state where mutual annihilation becomes a possibility."

Premier Nikita Khrushchev, though often blustery, understood this danger too. He ran into a major split with Red China on just this issue. "It is only a child or an idiot," he said, "who does not fear war." His successors, although they have condemned Khrushchev harshly for many of his acts, have not criticized him for avoiding nuclear war. The men of power in the Kremlin remain hard to live with, but they are realists; they know the dangers of annihilation that face the entire world.

Everything is not dark. During the first half-dozen years after World War II, many gloomy prophets predicted a third world war and a final holocaust. They believed that any serious local war would escalate to a nuclear war. And they thought that in times of crisis each side would feel an irresistible urge to strike the first blow with the aim of destroying the enemy's power to retaliate.

Since those predictions were made, we have experienced several wars in the Pacific basin, Central and South America, and the Middle East. And we have faced up to crises of a serious nature both at the Berlin Wall and in the installation of Cuban missiles. These experiences rank among the most perilous in history. But nobody used nuclear weapons or gave in to the urge to strike the devastating first blow.

There are two reasons why we have escaped the final holocaust thus far: *First,* the leaders of the United States and the Soviet Union understand the danger involved. It is inaccurate to say these leaders will sacrifice everything for the sake of power. Thus far, they have combined old maneuvers with a healthy caution.

And *second,* the United States, followed to some extent by the Soviet Union, has developed the invulnerable counterforce. Nuclear weapons in hardened underground silos or in submarines moving through the oceans will not be destroyed by the first attacks. The first strike loses its great advantage; anyone who delivers it knows he will be hit by a counterforce.

While no master stroke of diplomacy or futuristic defense system like Star Wars is going to make the world safe, there are many opportunities for the reasonable use of power. It seems that a good stance for a Christian may be to urge the combination of strength and restraint. It is possible for a country to maintain a nuclear deterrent so that no one will want to attack that country. Yet governments with nuclear power need not use that force to coerce others, even when the temptation to do so is great. It is possible to negotiate, to maintain patience, to endure irritations without unleashing nuclear destruction.

The responsibility of the public in world affairs. Although the leaders in a democratic society carry heavy responsibilities, they cannot solve everything. What they do depends to a large degree upon the intelligence and understanding of the citizens of the land.

Two characteristics of the American public make it difficult for leaders to exercise leadership.

First, Americans love to turn every conflict into a melodrama. They label the hero and the villain. Whatever the hero does is good, and whatever the villain does is bad. It is the business of the hero to lick the villain in a hard, though preferably a fair, fight.

One characteristic of a fight is that what is good for one fighter is bad for the other. Often we think of bargaining and negotiating in the same way. Anytime the other side gains, we lose. But this is not necessarily right thinking. Sometimes bargains are good for both sides. The art of negotiating is finding policies that benefit everybody. As long as the public insists on turning international policy into a melodrama and regarding all negotiation as weakness, they increase the perils of life in a perilous world.

The *second* quality that often misleads the American public has to do with the concept of revolution. This country, although born of a revolution, finds it hard to understand the revolutionary spirit that is loose in the world today. The drive for freedom and material independence is still high among nations that are underdeveloped.

Although the United States has only a little more than 9 percent of the free world's population and 8 percent of its area, its citizens consume nearly half of its materials. The per capita consumption of raw materials is roughly 10 times as high in the United States as the rest of the free world. But elsewhere, 10,000 people a day die of starvation or malnutrition, and more than half the world lives in continuous hunger.

How do faith and ethics fit into international politics? For the most part, nations act in terms of national interest. When there are collisions of interest, compromises are desirable. When ethics are involved, compromise becomes harder. A nation usually assumes that its cause is right and its enemy's cause is wrong. Then compromise seems shameful. If religion is added to the picture, the conflict becomes still more intense. Holy wars are the most fanatical of all wars. When people become convinced that God is on their side, defeat of the enemy becomes sacred, and compromise becomes disgraceful. But ethics and faith do not stay out of international problems, because they are part of any important human concern.

Crisis usually brings two opposite temptations. One is to succumb to futility, which wants to quit by asking the question, "What is the use?" The other is to assume an attitude of arrogance, which acts as though we can always have our way if we are only tough enough.

President Kennedy reflected on the world crisis in a television appearance not long before his death: "I think the problems are more difficult than I had imagined they were. Secondly, there is a limitation upon the ability of the United States to solve these problems. . . . I think our people get awfully impatient and maybe fatigued and tired, and are saying, 'We've been carrying this burden for 17 years. Can we lay it down?' We can't lay it down, and I don't see how we are going to lay it down in this century." Prolonged crisis requires that men bear burdens faithfully and morally, even though they know their actions will not resolve all their difficulties.

This last generation will certainly be remembered as the most destructive of all time. More people have been killed, more buildings destroyed, more refugees sent onto the road or into the water, and more national boundaries changed than during any other similar period of history.

In the name of defense we have burned enough oil to have run our tractors for 100 years. We have killed more people in the last 35 years than in any previous 1,000 years. We have destroyed 13 million homes in Europe and 17 million in Asia, leaving 40 million homeless, helpless refugees.

One news analyst said, "When we get through with exploiting our resources and exercising our utmost ingenuity in killing one another, at $1½ million a head, we ought to have enough brains to know how to help men live, and be able to show a profit in the operation."

There is no way to build a temple of peace without building it on the foundation of Jesus Christ and His gospel of love. The future Church can spread this love by recognizing the rights of others. We can be ready to understand the point of view of our enemies. And Christians can develop a willingness to sacrifice our own interest for the common good.

General Douglas MacArthur was addressing the Congress of the United States when he said, "Peace, in its final analysis, is a spiritual attainment." There is a close connection between our faith and our works. We have attempted to justify our society and make it appealing by maintaining a high standard of living instead of keeping a high regard for its spiritual foundations. Only as we bring our actions to turn upon moral and spiritual decisions can we build peace in our time—at home, in the county courthouse, the state legislature, the national government, or at international tables of negotiation.

In his book *God Still Speaks in the Space Age,* James Roy Smith tells about four pictures in the lobby of the Radio City Building in New York. The *first picture* shows primitive man with his bare hands painfully trying to get his livelihood from an unfriendly environment. In the *second picture* man has learned to make a crude tool with which to till the earth. He is beginning to develop some creature comforts. In the *third picture* he has become master of the machine, living in a thriving civilization. And in the *fourth picture* Jesus of Nazareth is seen on the side of a hill. Pressing up toward Him are great masses of men, women, and children of all nations and colors, with hope and expectation on their faces. And beneath the picture are these words: "Man's ultimate destiny depends not on whether he can learn any new lessons, or make new discoveries, but on his acceptance of the Lesson taught him close upon two thousand years ago."

Pastor Smith says he would like to suggest that there could also be a fifth picture. It could be an artist's impression of the words of Isaiah to the Space Age:

> It shall come to pass *in the latter days*
> that the mountain of *the house of the Lord*
> *shall be established as the highest of the mountains,*
> and shall be raised above the hills;
> and all the nations shall flow to it, . . .
> and *they shall beat their swords into plowshares,*
> and their *spears into pruning hooks;*
> nation shall *not lift up sword against nation,*
> neither shall they *learn war any more.*
> Isa. 2:2, 4, RSV

* * *

How can the future Church in the 20th century make a contribution toward peace? To begin with, we must understand that peace is a relative state and never will be known completely this side of heaven. Further, peace can also be known only in restricted areas. For instance, a home can become a place of peace. And so can a church, a business, or a community. And third, peace is not permanent, but ebbs and flows. Peace is localized and relative. But in spite of these limitations, there is a kind of peace that the future Church can represent.

First, Christians can focus on teaching and learning human values. Human beings are more than high-class animals dominated by the rhythms of hostility and sex. In the right atmosphere and with proper guidance, human beings can be led to the discovery of love, loyalty, forgiveness, commitment, dignity, and other human values. In fact, the final goal of all education is to teach men and women how to live together. Any educational system that fails to do this has failed, regardless of the amount of salable skill and knowledge learned by the student.

Second, the future Church can become an active leader in a stand against sin. Misdirected good is not the same as sin. Neither is deprivation. Sin is the innate tendency of human beings toward wrongness of attitude and behavior. Sin does not go away with time, nor will it disappear by being ignored. The only cure for sin is forgiveness and cleansing that comes by faith in Jesus Christ.

Third, the future Church can help build homes based on old-fashioned virtues. These virtues include so-called outmoded concepts including Sabbath Day observance, tithing, sacrifice, family prayers, hard work, individual responsibility, long-range goals, and a will to get along with each other. The home is still the nation's strongest bulwark of love and security. If the home is unstable and torn with strife, then our lives reflect that. When the home disintegrates, the nation disintegrates. And when the homes are strong, the nation is strong.

Fourth, the future Church can demonstrate the transforming love of Jesus Christ. Jesus Christ does not give you the power to join the church, keep the commandments, stay out of trouble, and be decent. He gives you the power to become a son of God, a transformed person, a new individual. The desire for peace on earth is inherent in man. War is a perversion that sin has brought upon the world. Was not Jesus prophesied to be the "Prince of Peace"? Was not the message of the angels that His coming would bring peace on earth to men of goodwill? The gospel of Jesus Christ is a gospel of peace—peace within and without. There is no movement toward peace that does not begin with the single individual who can have peace with God, peace with his family, peace with his neighbors, and peace within himself.

The greatest need of the 20th century is to find a way to build enduring peace in the world. Millions of Christians in the future churches of the world must play a central role in this process.

The best single thing that can be done by Christians who want peace on earth is to begin by living their faith in Jesus Christ. From one person, the love, tolerance, compassion, and motivation for good can be passed on to the uttermost parts of the earth. Perhaps the best way to close this book is to contemplate the prophetic words of Micah. Unlike Isaiah and Jeremiah, Micah lived in a small country town along the side of an international highway where he could watch the conquerors and the refugees go by. Here he heard the voice of the Lord similar to Isaiah's message:

But *in the last days* it shall come to pass,
that *the mountain of the house of the Lord
shall be established* in the top of the mountains,
and it shall be exalted above the hills;
and *people shall flow unto it.*
And *many nations shall come,*
and say, Come,
and let us go up to the mountain of the Lord,
and to the house of the God of Jacob;
and he will teach us of his ways,
and we will walk in his paths:
for the law shall go forth of Zion,
and the word of the Lord from Jerusalem.
And he shall judge among many people,
and rebuke strong nations afar off;
and *they shall beat their swords into plowshares,
and their spears into pruninghooks:
neither shall they learn war any more.*
But they shall sit every man under his vine
and under his fig tree;
and none shall make them afraid:
for the mouth of the Lord of hosts hath spoken it.
Mic. 4:1-4

The purpose of this chapter:
> To present a limited overview on the possibility of war and peace in our time and what the future Church can do about it.

QUESTIONS FOR THOUGHT AND DISCUSSION
1. In what ways is this "one world"?
2. Just how serious are world politics and why?
3. Why have we escaped a nuclear holocaust to date?
4. What responsibility does the Church have in world politics?
5. How do faith and ethics fit into international politics?
6. What is the ultimate route to peace in our time?